Quaker Parrot

Quaker Parrots as pets

Quaker Parrot Keeping, Pros and Cons, Care, Housing, Diet and Health.

by

Roger Rodendale

Table of Contents

Introduction

Without a doubt, Parrots make the most wonderful and loving companions. These birds are extremely intelligent and entertaining. Whether it is teaching them new tricks or even teaching them to talk, a Parrot is an absolute delight to have at home. They form strong bonds that will last for decades. Most Parrot species, especially the Quaker Parrot, will love all members of the family even when they are kept at home in pairs. The only thing that you need to do as a Quaker owner is learn as much as you can about these birds and try your best to give them a good life.

The thing with Parrots is that they have been domesticated by people only a few hundred years ago, unlike cats and dogs that have been our companions for several centuries. So, genetically, these creatures are not adapted to being domesticated. This means, you need to put in a lot of work and try to become your Parrot's flock instead of forcing him to be a member of your family. In simple words, you really need to work hard to make your Parrot accept you and your family. Once that has been done, you have a loyal companion for life.

Quaker Parrots, also known as Monk Parrots, can be quite a handful. Don't let their name fool you into believing that these creatures are calm and collected. They will wake you up from your deepest sleep, annoy your neighbors from time to time and even pull off the strangest antics to get your attention. But, the beauty of these Parrots is that there will never be a dull moment in your life if you successfully socialize them and raise them to be well behaved birds. It really depends upon how far you are willing to go to make your Parrot understand the dynamics of your life.

Parrots, as mentioned before, are highly intelligent. This gives you the advantage of being able to train them. If you are skilled enough with this bird, you can make sure that he is able to adapt to a routine set by you. The most important thing is to build trust and maintain it. Your Parrot should know that you mean no harm and are actually a part of his flock. After all, your home is a completely new environment for him. These creatures are thinkers which means that they will analyze your every move towards them. Unless your bird feels secure in your presence, you need to keep working towards it.

If you are new to the world of Parrots, this book is everything you need and more. You will get all the information that you need to raise a bird that is happy and healthy. The idea behind this book is to bring to you the experiences of several Parrot parents. That way, when you are facing an issue with your beloved bird, you know that it can be overcome with a little perseverance.

Chapter 1: My Quaker Parrot

These Parrots are considered the "perfect Parrots" to have because of their ability to socialize and their immense intelligence. They are known by several names such as the Quaker Parakeet, Monk Parakeet and Monk Parrot. You should not get confused with the term "Parakeet" that is often associated with these birds in literature. The reason for this is their long tail that closely resembles the tails of parakeets.

The name "Quaker" comes from the typical shaking of the body and the head. While it seems like the bird is distressed or upset when they exhibit this behavior, it is perfectly normal for Quaker Parrots. It almost seems like they are trying to get water out of their ears. But, it is not really certain why these birds exhibit this behavior.

a. Description

These birds are medium sized, growing up to an average of 11-13 inches. The wingspan of Quaker Parrots is generally about 48 cms and these birds will weigh about 100 grams. Female Quaker Parrots are smaller in size. On an average, they will be 10-20% smaller than a male. However, you can only determine the gender of your Quaker through DNA testing or feather testing. Both the male and the female are identical in appearance unlike other birds like the Eclectus Parrot that is sexually dimorphic, which means that the male and the female have distinct coloration that helps you tell them apart. Quaker Parrots do not weigh more than 100 grams.

These birds have rounded bodies that taper into a long tail. The head is also round and stout. Eyes are bright and placed close to the beak.

Coloration in these Parrots differ with the species. Of course, the most common birds that you will come across are the green Quakers. They are the nominate subspecies or the subspecies that were originally described. We will discuss the other subspecies in the following section.

As for the nominate subspecies, the boy is predominantly green. The forehead is usually a bluish grey color while the lores, cheeks and the throat are grey or pale grey in color. The breast feathers range from grey-brown to grey and have distinct markings. The nape, the back, the upper wing coverts and the crown are dark green in color. You will see a distinct tan band on the mod abdomen. An interesting yellow green coloration is seen in the lower back, rump and the thighs. The lower wing coverts and the lower area of the tail feathers are green or blue in color.

The beak is usually a pale brownish yellow color while the legs are a contrasting grey. Sometimes, the beak can also be a very bright orange shade. The iris of the Quaker Parrot is brown in color.

This natural plumage of the bird is great for camouflage in the wild. However, when you look at the domestic birds, hybridization has led to several shades besides the above mentioned green color. Of course, they also have distinct coloration that help us distinguish between one sub species and another.

b. Taxonomy and Classification

The Green Quaker that originates from Argentina and the neighboring South American countries is the most widely accepted bird from the genus Myiopsitta. It is categorized as Myiopsitta Monachus. This is the largest subspecies of this genus. There are four recognized subspecies that originate from different areas and are also physically quite unique when compared to the Quaker Parrot. One of these sub species, namely the Cliff Parakeet is one of the most debated ones as it has been categorized as a separate species and a sub species off and on. As of now, it has been included among the subspecies of this Parrot. The reason for this, as stated by the American Ornithologists' Union is that there isn't enough data that has been published with respect to this bird. The subspecies are:

- Myiopsitta Calita: This bird originates from the Andean foothills in the southwestern region of Bolivia and regions of northwestern Argentina and Paraguay. These birds are smaller than the Monachus subspecies. They do not have any blue coloration on the head but you will notice a small tinge of Blue on the abdomen.

- Myiopsitta Cotorra- You will find this bird in the areas ranging from Southwest Brazil all the way to Rio Paraguay. In the central basin of Parana and the Gran Chaco, as well, you should be able to find many members from this subspecies. These birds are smaller than the Calita subspecies. The brighter green plumage is distinctive to these birds. They have lesser yellow in comparison to the nominate species.

- Myiopsitta Luchsi- These birds are also called the Cliff Parakeet which is the center of debate as far as the classification is concerned. They are found in the central region of Bolivia in the Andean valley. Their distribution also extends to the southeastern parts of La Paz and the Northern parts of the Chuquisaca area. These birds have bright yellow underparts and lighter underwings. They do not have any scalloping on the breast region. Plumage is clearer in these birds and the maxilla also has a darker base.

You will see that the distribution of the first three species mentioned above meet in the region of Paraguay. The Cliff Parakeet on the other hand does not overlap in terms of the distribution. In any case, it is believed that the distinctness of all the three subspecies need to be evaluated a lot more.

All the subspecies mentioned above are Neotropical or new world Parrots. They have been known to the world only since Columbus noted down details of these birds in the 1400s. Most Parrots from this category, including the ones above are placed in the Arini tribe. These are the long tailed birds like the Macaws.

The monk Parrot or the nominate species is also available in Blue and White colorations. Many Parrot owners claim that the blue variety of these birds are very distinctly different in behavior although they belong to the same subspecies. Let us take a look at the differences in the next section.

c. Blue v/s Green Quaker

The two birds belong to the same family and subspecies but have very distinct personalities. So, if you are still contemplating about which one to bring home, here are a few differences that will help you decide which bird is best for you.

To begin with, Blue Quakers are smaller in size in comparison to Green Quakers. They are usually about 90-110 grams in size while the latter can be in the weight range of 110-130 grams. The Blue Quakers are also softer than the green ones. This means that they are prone to more health issues. However, feather plucking is less common in Blue Quakers. In fact, blue owners claim that their birds never pluck feathers.

In terms of personality, the green ones can be a little more "sassy". The blues are very sweet in nature and also quite mild. Of course, Green Quakers are also wonderful birds that are quite friendly. But, they will think and analyze more than the blue ones. Blues will easily go to anyone once they have been hand tamed. So, if you have a large family where everyone wants to pet the bird and play with it, the blues are a better option. They are a lot easier to handle.

Talking ability is definitely better in the Green Quakers. The blue ones will pick up words and phrases. However, they will not learn as much and as fast as the Green Quakers. Greens have also been known to use the words and human language in perfect context. This is an ability that you will not really find in the Blues. Of course, for those who want a very good talking Parrot, the Green Quaker is the best option.

These differences are based on the observations made by several Quaker owners. However, there are exceptions to the above differences. While there are distinct differences between green and blue birds, choosing one for your home depends entirely on the personality and the connection of one individual bird.

Do not approach any Quaker with preconceived ideas. This may leave you disappointed or overwhelmed. The personality of a bird is certainly influenced by the genetics. However, a large part also depends upon how you raise the bird and how the bird has been treated in the past. If your bird is well socialized and trained, he will become an essential part of your home, irrespective of whether he is blue or green.

c. Ecology

These Parrots are quite common across the globe. There was a great explosion in their population in South America because of the expansion of the Eucalyptus forests. This type of artificial forestry became popular for the production of paper pulp. Needless to say, the Quakers occupied trees in these forests and began to build nests. With no competition from other species, they began to thrive very well. These birds are, in fact, considered to be agricultural pests in several parts of the world including Brazil, Argentina and Uruguay. Cliff Parrots will trouble maize field owners occasionally but are not really considered pests.

You will find these birds as feral and self-sustaining populations in several parts of Europe and the United States of America. They also thrive in Canada, Brazil, Israel, Bahamas, Cayman Islands, Easter Islands, South Korea and Japan. These birds have been introduced in several parts of the world. Being woodland species, they are able to adapt to the urban setting quite easily.

In parts of the world where these birds have been introduced, it is feared that they may not only damage crops but also cause harm to the native species. Several people oppose killing of this bird because of their charismatic nature and the dispute about the status of this bird as a pest. In the UK, there is a plan to eradicate the wild Monk Parrots. This step taken by the Department of Environment, Food and Rural affairs is to protect crops and the local wildlife. However, in other parts of the world, this is not really an issue because the populations of these birds are smaller. It could also be possible that the urban population does not pose any threat to the agriculture of the area.

Feral populations are those that have descended from local, domesticated founder populations. As we have discussed before, Monk Parrots are very intelligent and highly social. This has led to the development of various dialects of vocalizations between different groups. They have also developed traditions that pertain to the area that they belong to. This sort of change in dialect is usually noticed when the founder population contains several birds. However, if these populations are smaller, the dialect shift may happen if the prominent members of the population have an unusual dialect. In the Milford Metropolitan Area in Connecticut, it has been noticed that there are over three different dialects.

Let us take a look at some parts of the world where these species have been introduced:

Brazil

Originally, these birds only occurred in the southern and south western regions of Brazil. However, recently an expansion of the population was observed all the way to Rio de Janeiro. Experts believe that this expansion is mainly due to birds that escaped the pet trade. You will find Quaker Parrots in the Aterro do Flamengo gardens in Brazil. Here, the birds occupy the palm trees. Birds in this region will also make nests in the leaves of the coconut palm trees.

You will also find these birds around the domestic terminal and the Santos Dumont Airport. Some communal nests have also been seen in the gardens of Quinta da Boa Vista. For a long time, escaped birds were reported in the Santa Catarina State. This gave rise to a feral colony in the Florianopolis area around the beginning of the 21st century. In fact, several birds were seen near the highway of the Rio Vermelho- Vargem Grande region.

Mexico

In Mexico, records of the Monk Parrot were first seen in the year 1999. There are records from various cities including Celaya, Tuxtla, Oaxaca, Puebla, Morelia, Hermosillo, Mexicali and Gutierrez. Some have also been seen at the mouth of River Loreto.

The nesting populations are mostly seen in Oaxaca and Mexico City. There are growing populations in the city of Puebla, mostly in the southern region. This is where most aviaries in the region are. These birds even visit aviaries and are seen clinging on to them. There are no studies to suggest what effects these birds have had on the local population of Green Parakeets.

After a ban was imposed on trading the local Parrot species, most Mexican traders turned to the Monk Parrot. This led to a lot of escapees. In fact, in Mexico, the breast and head feathers of the Monk Parrots have often been dyed yellow to pass them off as an endangered species from the Amazon. The range of Monk Parrots in Mexico spreads across seven cities that are quite far from one another. This indicates that the birds must have escaped from traders and formed small populations around these areas.

United States

In the late 1900s, Monk Parrots were first brought to the USA as pets. Some escaped while some were released, leading to several feral populations. In less than 10 decades of being introduced there, there were established populations of these birds in seven states. Today, close to 100,000 birds are seen in the area of Florida alone.

These birds are also able to survive cold temperatures. As a result, they have formed colonies even in placed like Chicago, Dallas, New York, New Jersey, Edgewater, Louisville, Massachusetts, Rhode Island and the Southern region of Washington. Being so hardy, these birds are among the most successful birds to be introduced in this region.

In the year 2012, it was seen that a pair of Monk Parrots attempted to make a nest in New York. Just before the egg was laid, this nest was removed over concerns about a fire due the proximity to an electric transformer.

In addition to this, accidental releases also improved populations of this bird in Brooklyn in the Green Wood Cemetery. Initially the crew members tried to remove their nests but stopped doing so after they realized the role of these birds in actually protecting the area. The nests of Monk Parrots led to a reduction in the number of Pigeons in the region. The feces of Pigeons contained chemicals that could harm the ancient structure while the feces of the Monk Parrot did no such damage. Today, the bird is an unofficial mascot of Brooklyn College. There are also several birds in the Bronx area. These birds predominantly live in the lamp posts. It is believed that these populations are the result of pet trade shipments that came from Argentina.

In Chicago, it is believed that these birds escaped from O'Hare airport while being smuggled into the country. After surviving the harsh winter conditions, these birds thrived in this region from the 1960s till date. Healthy populations of close to 100 birds have been seen in the parks around Chicago. These birds were also part of a large ornithological study conducted in the year 2012.

Europe

You will mostly find these birds in the Canary Islands, Valencia, Tarragona, Roquetas de Mar, Zaragoza, Barcelona, Madrid,

Seville, Cadiz, Torremolinos and the Balearic Islands. These birds were sighted in the year 1985 for the first time in this region. They are usually seen in the Complutense University Campus in Madrid. They are also frequently seen in Casa de Campo. In Barcelona, they are often seen in parks in numbers as large as the pigeon populations. The urban parks with palm trees and grass areas are very popular among these birds. They also prefer parks that are closer to the sea or a river. They are an invasive species because of which they have become a potential threat to local fauna including sparrows and pigeons. Of course, magpies are hardier and have not been affected so far. These birds have also caused a lot of damage in the agricultural belt of Europe. You will find the largest population of Parakeets in Europe in Barcelona. Close to 2500 Parrots have been seen there as of 2013.

The population of these birds in the UK is relatively small. In the Home Counties region about 150 birds had been seen in the year 2011. However, by the regulation of the Department of Education, Food and Rural Affairs, there is a plan to control the population of these birds. They have caused ample damage to the native bird species, the infrastructure, as well as the crops.

d. Nesting Behavior

The most distinctive thing about a Quaker Parrot is the nesting behavior. These are the only Parrot species that actually build nests using sticks. These nests are either built in trees or in manmade structures in the urban habitats. Most Parrots will just use holes in trees as their nests.

But, the Quaker Parrot is different. This bird is extremely intelligent and tactful. According to members of the Quaker Parakeet society, these birds have a natural desire to make a home and keep it. Their nests are very large and dome shaped. The nest is built using several clusters of sticks. Now these nests actually contain several compartments or chambers. Each chamber is used by one pair of birds to breed and roost. This is almost like the apartments that are built by people.

Quaker Parrots live in large colonies in the wild. Breeding is also colonial in these birds. These large nests with multiple chambers actually have separate entrances to let each pair of bird in. Studies have shown that these birds can build nests as large as some small automobiles known to man. Sometimes, these nests will also attract other occupants including preying birds such as the spot winged falconet. Some species of Ducks and Mammals also occupy these nests.

These birds show great community spirit. They love to interact with their neighbors. In fact, after a clutch of eggs have hatched, the parent birds will have helpers. These helpers are other pairs of birds that will help the parents feed the hatchlings. This behavior is rarely seen in other Parrot species. It is this spirit that also makes these birds wonderful pets. Their love for interaction keeps them close to their human family and also makes them very social towards other people. That does not mean that you can just reach in and pick your bird up.

Quaker Parrots can become extremely territorial. Several owners have been bitten or attacked for reaching into the cage of the bird without warning. This happens even when there is no nest in the cage. It is true even in the case of the most gentle and meek bird. However, it is unfair to generalize this behavior as some birds could even be completely open about their cage. Even if your Quaker does attack you, do not assume that it is the fault of the bird. Avoid catching them off guard or they will only display their most instinctive reaction.

When kept as pets, these birds do not have enough room to build these large nests in the cage. However, they will never stop trying. They will pick up anything that is remotely close to a stick or thread and will try to build and weave a nest. This is one of the most entertaining behaviors displayed by the Quaker Parrot.

This also means that these birds will take anything that they find. They will carry objects that they like back to the cage and actually arrange them in the cage. Some Parrot owners say that their birds have developed an inclination towards pens. Since they resemble sticks, all pens will be taken back to the cage and used as part of the cage.

People have retrieved all sorts of items from the cage of their Parrot including forks, pencils, letter openers etc. In fact, one Quaker owner also recalls how his bird had made away with his eyeglasses. They were on the table one moment and were gone the next. Now the unsuspecting man had to make do with his prescription glasses until the original ones were found in the cage of the Quaker.

e. Distribution and Habitat

These birds are usually found near areas with large water bodies. They are native to the lowland regions in Brazil, Argentina, Paraguay, Bolivia and Brazil. These birds will be found in the open savannas, palm groves and the scrub forests. Basically, any region with low rainfall is preferred by these birds. They are also seen in city parks, yards and farms in South America.

These birds are extremely adaptable. As a result, they are also able to occupy Eucalyptus trees. As discussed before, they can build complex nests in the area that they choose to live in. This includes urban manmade structures.

The terrestrial biomes of these birds include scrub forests that are mostly found in regions with long dry seasons. They are also found in the grasslands and savannas. A savanna is basically a grasslands that has trees scattered around or even clumps of trees scattered around. They lie somewhere in between a forest and a grassland. Tropical Savannas contain several trees that are scattered around a region without really forming a canopy. These savannas are usually found in Australia, Africa and South America. You also have temperate grasslands that consist of mostly grass which differs in species and height. The vegetation in these regions depend largely on the amount of moisture that us available.

f. Food Habits

Quaker Parrots are omnivorous in the wild. Their diet consists of a wide range of foods including leaf buds, thistles, grasses, parts of trees, fruits, seeds, blossoms, insects etc. These birds will consume a large variety of seeds but prefer stiped and black sunflower seeds or pumpkin seeds. Any small seed is welcome with these birds. In the highly populated areas, it has been noted that these birds consume legumes, drying meat, cereal crops like maize and sorghum. They also consume citrus crops. It is this love for crops that has earned them the reputation of being a pest. This is not confirmed, however. But in many parts of the world the population of this bird has been curbed to ensure that they do not cause further damage to property.

g. Personality and Behavior

Quaker Parrots are among the most intelligent birds known to people. The complex colonial behavior and nest construction is enough proof that these birds are highly sophisticated mentally. Their speaking ability has made this bird more popular among pet owners. With a regular routine, these birds can even learn to sing complete songs.

These birds are extremely active and playful. They love to use toys and will actually figure out ways to entertain themselves with whatever resources are available. They are not really acrobatic in comparison to other birds in this species. However, their fun nature and great sense of humor makes these birds wonderful companions. These birds can be very picky, however. Some Quaker owners will tell you that their birds will never play with a toy. This is possibly because toys have been introduced very late to these birds. It is important for you to make sure that your bird gets plenty of toys at a young age. Otherwise, do not be surprised if he chooses to shout or talk to entertain himself.

These birds are fearless and highly social. That is why they do not really shy away from people and will live with them easily. This explains the wide urban distribution of Quaker Parrots. These

17

birds are also curios by nature and will analyze every situation and object.

Overall, Quaker Parrots are very pleasant beings that make wonderful companions. These birds will get attached to every member of your family and will become a part of your home before you realize.

Chapter 2: The Quaker and Other Birds

When you are bringing home a pet bird, it is very hard to decide which bird is perfect for you. There are so many Parrot species out there that it can be confusing to most new pet owners. In this chapter, we will discuss the differences between Quaker Parrots and other commonly domesticated Parrot species.

a. Quaker v/s Sun Conures

These are the two most popular Parrot species across the globe. There are some specific personality differences that will help you decide which one is a better option for your home.

To begin with, Conures are not the best talkers. They cannot speak as clearly as the Quaker birds. In fact, Quakers will also learn to associate words with the context and speak very well. For instance, when you give your bird your hand to step up on, he will say "Step up" before actually climbing up. Some Quakers pick up simple words like "Hello" even before they are weaned. With Conures, you will have to give them at least 6 months before they learn to say any words that they hear.

Quakers are known to be feistier with a nice attitude that is just natural to them. On the other hand, Conures tend to be slower. For instance, the biting pattern of a Quaker bird is generally a fast nip. On the other hand, a Conure will hand on to the finger that they bite. Conures are more open to other birds and are milder. On the other hand, Quaker birds do not get along very well with other birds unless they are introduced at a very young age. In fact, it seems like these birds love to tease other birds.

Quaker birds also laugh like the Macaws. They will also develop fun games that they will play with you. However, they will only play these games when they know that someone else is watch you. In that sense, Quakers are attention seekers.

These birds will eat just about anything you feed them. Sun Conures on the other hand are fussier when it comes to eating. They pick their favorites and will seldom eat foods that they do not pick themselves. A Quaker just needs to see you eating a certain food and they will eat it up without any complaint.

Quaker birds are known to be clever, more curious and more prone to escaping than Conures. These birds learn really fast and can even learn to let themselves out of a cage if they want to. Sun Conures are sweeter birds and are more good natured. So, if you really look at the differences, you can say that the Quaker is funny and clever while the Conure is funny and sweet. The bird that you choose really depends upon your personality. If you think that you can keep up with the antics of a Quaker, it is the best bird for you.

b. Quakers v/s Bourke Parrots

Bourke Parrots are, of course, physically very different from Quaker Parrots. They are more colorful and very beautiful birds. In comparison to the Quaker birds, they are a lot quieter. They do not screech or scream for attention as much as your Quaker bird would.

On the flipside, they are not very good talkers like the Quaker Parrots. They normally don't talk and the words that they do pick up are not uttered very clearly. Basically, they are not as great as mimicking human speech as the Quaker birds. The latter are really fast learners and will pick up several words and phrases.

The personality of the Quaker bird is what makes it so popular across the world. These birds have such an interesting and queer attitude. They just seem to have a lot more enthusiasm in them than most other Parrots. Some Parrot owners will tell you how funny and entertaining these birds can be. The Bourke Parrot however, is a mild and gentle bird. They are capable of staying quiet for several hours on end. They are also a lot calmer in comparison to the Quaker. The Quaker Parrot is more like a teenager while the Bourke Parrot is like a young adult, if we were to compare them to human beings!

That said, Quaker Parrots are often not recommended for people who have absolutely no experience with birds. They are harder to handle because of their usually territorial personality. So, if you are a first timer, a Bourke Parrot is a better option for you as these birds are more gentle and manageable. For kids, especially, a Bourke Parrot is a much safer option as they do not really get too edgy or inquisitive like a Quaker. Most often, a Quaker's curious nature is misinterpreted as being aggressive.

c. Quaker Parrots v/s Senegals

Quaker Parrots are not exactly cuddlers like the Senegals. They are not so fond of being touched and handled and can get a little nippy if they are not too pleased. On the other hand, Senegals love to be touched and cuddled and will respond to you in the most positive manner when you stroke their cheek or gently caress their little heads. With a Quaker, it really depends on how well you have managed to socialize your bird and made him accustomed to people and their touch.

Senegals are quiet birds in comparison to the Quaker birds. The latter can be very talkative and vocal. They love to chatter with their human family and will tell you everything that they want to about their day. Senegals are not so vocal. They may have rare outbursts or calls and nothing more.

In terms of talking and mimicking speech, Quakers are definitely way ahead of the Senegals. They are able to pick up several words and sentences quite easily. That is not the case with Senegals who are less prone to talking. They may pick up a few words but are unable to talk as clearly as the Quakers. Another interesting thing with Senegals is that their ability to speak is very individualistic. Some birds that do learn to speak will have excellent vocabulary. But most often, they will not really talk as well as Quakers or other species of Parrots that are known for their mimicry skills.

Quaker Parrots are extremely active birds. They love to play, collect things from around the house and hoard them in the cage and just meddle around. Senegals are less active. They like to sit or perch in the nest without being disturbed. Quakers are certainly a lot more entertaining and playful in comparison to the Senagal.

As we have mentioned before, Quaker Parrots are excellent socially. Their natural instinct to stay in large colonies, makes them better adjusted to human families as well. They are able to get along with almost every member of the family if they have been socialized well. However, senegals tend to bond with only one person in the family. They may or may not be as friendly with other people in the family as the Quakers. They are also a lot more nervous around people. Quakers, on the other hand are fearless birds. Their inquisitive nature makes them want to be around people and actually learn their ways. They may even develop small rituals with their owners and family.

These differences between different species of birds are very generalized. You need to understand that every bird is an individual. So when you are choosing a bird for your home, make sure that you understand how much time you can spend with him. If you are able to give them the time that they need, they can learn all the habits that you want them to learn.

If not, their instinctive behavior will kick in and they will display the same behavior that they do in the wild. The reason that birds get nippy sometimes is the fact that they are prey animals out there in the wild. They need to be defensive and will always take care of themselves. If they do not trust you enough, they are likely to either get scared or aggressive.

The key to having a happy Parrot at home is spending a lot of time with them. With Quaker Parrots especially, the more time you spend with them as babies, the more they are going to get friendly with you and your social circle.

In the end, it all depends upon where you have brought your bird home from, the kind of handling, breeding and training that the bird has undergone in the early years and the sense of security that you are able to provide your bird with in this time. The next chapter tells you exactly how you can choose a bird for your home. You will also get specific details on choosing which place you want to bring your bird from. These factors are the most important in determining your experiences with your bird.

Chapter 3: Choosing the Perfect Companion

There is a certain chemistry involved with the bird that you finally decide to bring home, no doubt. You just see a bird and know that he is the one you want to take home. However, you also need to know where to look and how to make sure that your bird is coming from a reliable source.

The experiences of your bird in his initial years will determine how much he trusts you and how well behaved he will be in your home. Health is also a major factor when it comes to deciding which bird you want to bring home. So, the first step is to choose the most reliable source for your bird.

a. Buying a Parrot

There are three common sources for pet owners to get their bird home from- the breeder, a pet store and a rescue shelter. Each one has its own pros and cons. If you are able to figure out which one works best for you, half your job is done. Here are some simple things to watch out for when you are shopping around for a new bird.

1. Choosing a good breeder

There are two kinds of breeders that you will come across- commercial breeders and hobby breeders. Commercial breeders will produce chicks in large numbers and are considered very inhumane due to the unethical breeding practices. These people cannot guarantee the health of the bird and may not even be able to support you in your journey with your Quaker.

Now, if you choose a hobby breeder, you will notice that they usually specialize in one type of bird or one type of hybrid even. These people are genuinely interested in raising Quaker Parrots and will usually do a lot of research about the bird. They will become a reliable source of information and knowledge whenever you have any doubts about your Quaker Parrot. Here are a few things that will tell you if your breeder is good enough or not:

- **The experience:** The breeder should have had ample experience with Quaker Parrots. Even if he or she is new to the world of breeding, they will know a lot about Quaker birds, their behavior, the breeding patterns etc. The more experience your breeder has with birds, the more likely he is to take good care of the birds to ensure top health. When you talk to a breeder, you will be able to know if he or she is genuinely passionate about the bird or if they are simply here to make a few fast bucks.

- **Willingness to answer queries:** Every good breeder knows that it is hard for anyone to buy a bird without asking questions. If your breeder is patient and kind, then it means that they will also be able to assist you in the future if you have any issues with your bird. They will also be able to answer clearly and logically because of the immense knowledge that they have about the bird in question.

- **Good Quarantining measures:** All good breeders will take extra care before introducing a new bird into the aviary because they are aware of the diseases that new birds could be carrying. This is a potential hazard to all the birds in the aviary. In fact, some breeders follow a closed aviary practice. This means that they will not allow new birds to be brought to the aviary at all. This is the best place to buy your bird from as they are less prone to infections from their cage mates.

- **Socialization efforts:** Hobby breeders usually have their aviary in their backyard. It is good to choose a breeder who lives with an active household. This includes a few pets and a family. That way, your bird is exposed to a lot of new experiences in the younger days. As a result, the bird is more social and is less prone to stress. While Quaker Parrots are resilient to stress by nature, having a bird who is good with people and pets makes it easier for you to handle them and take good care of them when they come into your home.

- **Weans the birds at ease:** A good breeder will give the babies ample time to wean. Weaning refers to the birds being able to eat on their own without help from the breeder or its parents. If the breeder will give you a date for weaning, it is not a good sign. They should be willing to take the time to wean the bird before sending them home with you. You can spend time with your bird in this period to make sure that he is accustomed to you.

- **Does not clip the feathers too early:** The first clip of the flight feathers is called a baby clip. This should only be done after the bird is weaned and ready to go home with you. If the flight feathers are clipped off very soon, there are chances that your bird will develop several emotional and behavioral problems that you will have to deal with when you bring him home. The quality of your pet is also highly compromised when the breeder is in a hurry to have the wings clipped off.

- **Connects you to past clients:** If the breeder is not sure about connecting you with previous owners, then there is some sign of insecurity on the breeder's part. Most breeders who have been in the business of raising birds will also be proud to take you along to visit the birds that have been bred by them. This is a sign of great confidence in the quality of the birds.

- **Provides a health guarantee**: You should be able to get a health guarantee for your bird in print. This health guarantee tells you that your bird is of top quality and that any issue that you face with the bird is the responsibility of the breeder. This is especially important if you are having the birds shipped in to your home.

2. Choosing a pet store

Pet stores are a lot more convenient as you will find several of them close to your home. But you need to understand that Quaker Parrots are exotic species and not every pet store is able to provide good care for these birds. You need to make sure that you are bringing home a healthy and happy bird. For this, the pet store that you choose should be able to give you a good quality bird. Here are a few tips to select a good pet store:

- **Cleanliness:** The pet store should not have an unpleasant odor when you walk in. Of course, you will be able to smell the fur and feathers but if you want to close your nose as soon as you enter, it means that the animals have not been maintained properly. The cages should not be jammed close to one another. They should be arranged in such a way that you can navigate through the store and look at the animals that have been kept there for sale.
- **The Animals and Birds:** If you find painted or dyed fish in the store, it is a commercial space that you want to run from. Also, it is very unusual for a pet store to have birds and reptiles together. This is because each of them requires a lot of care individually. Unless you have enough employees to take care of these creatures, it is impossible to provide good care. So if your pet store sells a Quaker and a reptile, you must make sure that you ask them how they manage to take care both creatures efficiently.
- **Willingness to help:** The staff at the pet store should be willing to help you look around and choose a bird for yourself. They should be able to answer your queries clearly and should not beat around the bush. Also observe the way they talk about the animals in their store. If they are belittling another bird or animal because it is less expensive than your Quaker, they are only trying to make a sale. They should also be able to handle the birds easily and should be gentle while doing so. This shows that they spend time with the animals and interact with them.
- **Will provide health guarantee:** A pet store that provides a health guarantee is definitely the best. They are absolutely sure about the quality of animals and birds in their store and will, therefore, give you a written guarantee. The duration of this guarantee is usually shorter than the one you can get from a breeder. You must certainly ask for a guarantee or contract when you are having the birds shipped.

You can also ask them about how they quarantine birds and how they handle birds from different sources. If this is a regular practice, it means that your birds are most likely to be healthy.

3. Is the bird healthy?

The ambience of the bird will tell you a lot about the health of the bird. It will also tell you if the birds have been cared for properly or not. If you see the following at a pet store or the breeder's, you need to make sure that you start looking for more options immediately:

- **The cage is unclean:** If the cage is poorly maintained, it is a definite red flag. You will notice feathers stuck to the grill. If there is dried poop on the floor of the cage, it means that the cage is not cleaned on a regular basis. The water bowl should have clean water. If you notice droppings in the food bowl or the water bowl, it means that the birds are not well maintained. Any good pet store or breeder will know that most avian diseases are spread due to unclean conditions that the bird grow in. They will try to maintain the best standards as far as sanitation and cage maintenance are concerned.

- **The bird is only given seeds:** There are two important reasons why you must avoid a breeder or pet store that only gives the birds seeds. First, it is very difficult to change the diet of your bird to a healthier one. Second, birds that eat only seeds may have severe nutritional deficiencies that can make the bird prone to infections and several unwanted diseases. Ideally, the bird should be given a variety of foods in order to remain healthy. They must get fruits and vegetables along with pellets as part of their diet. If a peek into the food bowl is not good enough for you to understand the actual diet of the bird, you can quiz the pet store owner or the breeder.

- **The bird is not active:** Birds are always very alert. Being prey animals, this is their natural disposition. When you approach the cage, the bird should respond in some way. Their posture will become erect, they will lean in towards you to understand who you are or they will at least fly away to a hiding spot. On the other hand if the bird is lethargic and unresponsive, it is a sign of poor health. Also look out for signs like improper feather growth, a ruffled appearance, bald spots, abnormal growth of the beak, scaly growths on the feet, matted feather near the cloaca and any discharge from the nasal or oral cavity. These are symptoms of poor health.

The health of the bird is the most important factor in deciding if you want to bring him home or not. Of course, you have to worry about the additional care an unwell bird will demand. It also means that the bird has not been given positive experiences in the growing years. Being in an unclean environment and not getting enough attention can be stressful for birds leading to unwanted behavioral issues like aggression or extreme fear.

4. What is a health guarantee?

A health guarantee is an assurance of sorts provided by the breeder or the pet store. It shows that they are confident enough about the quality of the bird to give you a guarantee against it. Now, a health guarantee is only valid if your bird has been tested by an avian vet within 72 hours of you taking the bird home. If your breeder insists that you see a specific vet, it is a cause for worry as they may have some mutual understanding. You will get a guarantee after the doctor confirms that the bird does not have any health issues.

A health guarantee will have a few terms and conditions that you need to read very carefully. Here are some of the common clauses that you will find in a health guarantee.

- The bird must be thoroughly examined by an avian vet with 72 hours of purchase.
- The guarantee does not cover any veterinary costs.
- In case the bird is diagnosed with any health issue in the first check-up, the pet store or breeder will replace the bird or will pay you back the entire amount that you paid for the bird.
- Any injury caused to the bird under your care is not covered by a health guarantee.
- Any health issues caused to the bird under your care is not covered by a health guarantee. This includes any form of stress, irresponsible husbandry, ill treatment of the bird and accidents

- Behavioral issues and psychological issues are not covered by the health guarantee.
- Any purchases you make while buying the bird such as cage and food is not included in the refund. You will only get a refund that is limited to the price that you paid to buy the bird.

Normally, Parrot health guarantees are valid for a period of 90 days. In this time, if the bird develops any problems despite proper health care, the money, or a portion of it, is returned to you. The later you take the bird to the vet, the lesser refund you get. For instance, if you return the bird after 3 days, you will get 70% back on the initial price of the bird. It you return the bird after 5-6 days, you will get 50% and so on. This is done to ensure complete fairness to both the owner and the breeder or the pet store owner.

Remember that a health guarantee is very different from a health certificate. The latter is necessary to obtain a license to keep your bird at home. You may also require it if you decide to travel with your bird. A health certificate will be given to you by a vet. Some breeders and pet stores also offer a health certificate at an additional cost of up to $80. This is an important document. So make sure that you get one along with a health guarantee. Some pet stores may not give you a health guarantee, although it is preferable if they do. However, with a breeder, a health guarantee is a most.

b. Adopting a Parrot

Adoption is the next option available when you decide that you want to bring home a pet Parrot. There are thousands of birds that need new homes. Some of them are given away when their owners are unable to take good care of them. Others are rescued from homes that are abusive for the bird. So, if you are able to afford good care and have the time to spend with these birds, adoption is one of the best ways to bring home a Quaker.

You could look for local rescue homes and see if any of them have a Quaker Parrot up for adoption. If not, you can look up websites like birdadoption.org or featherme.com that will give you a list of adoption centers near your home where you can possibly find a Quaker Parrot.

1. The truth about adoption

Adoption is not as easy as it sounds. It is not just about bringing the bird home from a rescue shelter and keeping him in a pretty cage. There is a lot of work that needs to be done from your end because these birds are most likely to be extremely stressed. That, in turn makes training and socializing the bird harder than it would be with a bird that is young and straight out of a secure nest. So, before you adopt a bird, here are a few things that you need to keep in mind.

- **The bird comes with baggage:** When birds need rehoming, there are chances that the bird has had past experiences that are pleasant or not so pleasant. In any case, the whole process of shifting homes is very traumatic and stressful for birds. When adopting from a reputed rescue center, the staff will be able to give you a brief history of the bird's life and will also tell you how you can deal with the problems that you may encounter. This is a good thing as you will receive enough education about the personality and the specific requirements of a certain bird.

- **Birds can change over time:** When you adopt a baby bird, you may feel like his personality is very mild and friendly. However, there is no guarantee that the personality will remain the same when the bird reaches sexual maturity. Some of them may become aggressive or shy depending upon their individual personality. So, always be prepared. If you are new to the world of Parrots, having someone who can help you cope with these issues is a good idea always.

- **It is a financial commitment:** Bringing home a bird that is injured or has any history of abuse is a big financial commitment. You will have to make regular visits to the vet to ensure that your bird is in top health at all times. The medicines that you need to buy for your bird are a big investment, too. Only when you are ready to take that on should you adopt a bird.

- **You need to make time:** With a bird who is recovering in your home, you cannot leave him alone all the time. The fact that he was neglected has led to the stress and the health issues in the first place. If the bird has been given up by a loving home because they were unable to care for it, it is even worse as the bird must have created strong bonds already. This is especially true for wonderfully social birds like the Quaker. If you are busy and do not have the time to bond with your bird and build the required trust, you must definitely not adopt one.

2. The adoption process

Once you are able to commit to the care and wellbeing of an adopted bird, you can begin the adoption process. It is quite simple. In reputed rescue centers, you will have to pay an adoption fee towards the bird that you bring home. This is a good investment as all good rescue centers will provide you with the following:

- An adoption application that will give you all the details that you need about the bird.
- Classes on avian health and Parrot care. If your bird has any specific needs, you may get additional classes as well.
- Three visits to the bird that you want to take home before you actually file the application. This is decent bonding time to help you understand the personality of the bird.
- A home visit from the authorities at the adoption center for safety and cage approval.

3. Your commitment as the adopter

You also have to take ample care of the bird. If you fail to do so, the rescue center may take the bird back. You have a few obligations as the adopter including:

- Complete check up by an avian vet of the other birds that you have at home within 12 months of adopting a new bird. This test must be negative for psittacosis.
- No breeding of the adopted bird.

- Safety of the bird when he is outdoors. You will have to use a harness or a flight cage when you take the bird outside.
- Provision of a smoke free environment for the bird. If you are a smoker, chances are that you may not get a Parrot to take home.
- Annual examination by an approved avian veterinarian.
- Provision of a good diet that includes fresh fruits and vegetables and good quality pellets.

The adoption fee for a Quaker is usually about $150 or £75. You will have to allow home visits by the authorities of the adoption center whenever required. If your home has aggressive pets that have attacked any bird in the past, you will have to surrender the bird. Some also have policies on the number of birds that can be kept in a home. In most rescue centers, you will not be allowed to adopt more than two birds in a span of 12 months. If the rescue center has any reason to believe that your home is inadequate for a Quaker Parrot, you will have to surrender him immediately.

Chapter 4: Bringing the Birdie Home

Once you have chosen the bird, the next challenge is to bring the bird home. It may seem as easy as putting the cage in your car and driving home. However, that is not true. The whole experience of travelling or being transported is not really very exciting for a bird. So, you need to make sure that you keep him as calm as possible. Now there are two transportation possibilities:

1. You drive the bird home
2. The bird is shipped to your home

Both these cases are unique and you need to understand how to manage a bird in either situation.

a. Driving a bird home

A drive is a very unique experience for a bird. Most often, a bird will find this very stressful because of the moving objects, the colors and all the sights and sounds. This may seem very ordinary to you but for a bird it can actually be very traumatic.

It is a good idea to purchase a temporary travel cage that you can even use in the future for vet visits. This will keep your bird secure throughout the drive. Place the cage securely on the seat and strap it in. Make sure that the floor is lined with paper or any other substrate. []You also need to keep some treats and water available to the bird. If your breeder or pet store is able to give you one of the bird's toys, it is a good idea as he will have something familiar during this new experience.

Do not talk to the bird when you are driving home. It is a good idea to go individually and not as a group when you buy the bird. New human voices are very disturbing for the bird. If you go as a group, there will be several new voices that will stress the bird out even more. Make sure that you do not play any music throughout the drive. Basically, you will avoid any additional surprises for the bird.

Keep the air-conditioner on in the car and set it to room temperature. It could be slightly lower on a hot day. In case your home is a long drive from the breeder's, it is a good idea to take a break every half an hour. A ten minute break is good enough for the bird to calm himself down and probably eat and drink a little. They may not even poop in a moving vehicle and become very uncomfortable if you do not give them a break.

b. The bird is shipped

No breeder will ship the bird to your doorstep. You will either have to collect the bird from the local post office or the airport. Remember that not all birds can be shipped through the postal service. It also depends on the regulations in your state. If your Quaker has been shipped using a freight service, it is a lot more stressful as the airport is busier and noisier than a post office.

Usually a bird is shipped within a week of making the payment. If the bird is being shipped with a freight service, you can ask for a specific date to collect your bird from the airport and he will be shipped accordingly. Once the bird has been shipped, you will be notified. You can contact the fright company to figure out how much time it will take for the package to arrive.

When you go to collect the box, you must take a small transfer cage along. The box will normally have a trap door. This will be marked with the words "Live bird". Open this door and place it before the door of your bird's cage. Let the bird take his time to walk into the transfer cage.

When you are getting a bird shipped to your house, you will have to do a little bit of homework. Ask the breeder or the store what the bird is accustomed to eating. Make sure this food is available to the bird in large quantities when he arrives. Do not try to change the diet on the day he arrives as he is already very stressed. You also need to give him clean drinking water using a bottle, preferably. Make sure the food and water is visible to the bird. Don't assume that he will go to the food if it is in the cage.

There are chances that your bird is sick. So you will drive him to the vet before you take him home. Make sure that he is certified as healthy. That way you will not have to worry about any critical illness in the future. During the bird's first drive with you, make sure you follow all the instructions given above.

In case of death while shipping, you may contact your breeder. You will most likely not get a refund but it is good to inform him of the situation.

It is advised that you drive the bird home yourself. Look for a breeder who is closer to where you live. Even if it is a longer drive, it is safer for you to collect your bird. During the flight to your home, there are chances that the bird will come in contact with toxins, very hot or warm conditions, dust and other conditions that can severely affect his health.

c. The first day

The first day of your bird in your home is very critical. In fact, the first week is very important to help the bird create positive associations with his new space. If not, there are chances that he will take longer to build trust and bond with you and your family.

The first thing you need to do is make sure that the bird is allowed to calm down. You need to prepare his new enclosure. Place it in a room that is rather quiet. This room should be away from any main road where there could be a lot of noise due to traffic. The bird must feel secure. So, place this cage against a wall. Do not keep it in an area like the hallway as there is too much commotion. You definitely do not want to place it in the family room or the living room. The bird should be in a space that allows him to observe his new home and family without really getting in the middle of all the action.

Make plenty of food available for the bird. Keep fresh water in the cage too. The first day should not include any interaction. As a new pet owner, you may be excited to fondle and cuddle the bird. But, it will only damage the health of your bird. Just walk past his cage, follow your normal routine but do not talk to him or interact with him.

You must make sure that you keep children away from the cage for the first few days. They will not tease or play with the bird. No loud music or television should be allowed in the house till the bird is at ease. You definitely do not want any visitors in your home. If there are any large and colorful objects in the room that you have placed the cage in, take it out immediately. If your home has multiple birds or other pets, you will not introduce them to the new bird. The new bird needs to be left alone.

It is a good idea to cover one part of the cage with a towel. This can become the bird's hiding place or sleeping area. It will also protect him from the light of the television and any other light in your home.

The next morning, you can simply change the food and water in the cage. Do not talk to the bird still. Just casually go about the cleaning and feeding and let your bird observe you. A bird that is already socialized will probably not be afraid of you. However, if your bird is reclusive and in one corner of the cage, he is probably still scared.

The most important thing to do would be to prepare your family and tell them that they will have to let the bird get acclimatized before they interact with the new member of the family. It is also a good idea to bring the bird home when you are in all day. Do not bring him if you know that he is going to be all alone on a particular day. That will only scare him a lot more in this brand new environment. While there should not be any interaction, the bird should be able to watch and observe your family.

d. Progressive interaction

For the next week, try to talk as little as you can to your Parrot. Keep socialization to a minimum. This means that you will not host parties or have people over for at least one week after the Parrot arrives. You also need to keep noises like the TV and radio at a minimum.

Make sure you pass by the cage often. That way, your bird will get accustomed to your presence. You will also be interacting with the bird when you are feeding him and cleaning the cage. This is the bonding time.

After a day or two, you can say words like "Hello" and "Bye" in a very soft and soothing voice. With a Quaker, do not be surprised if he responds with the same words.

Once you think that the bird is ready, you can start actual interaction. You will know that your bird is ready by observing his body language. His posture will be erect. He will use the perch. His level of activity will increase. Also, when you approach the cage to feed him, he will not cover himself or retreat behind the towel. That indicates that your bird is getting used to your home. With Quaker birds, this will happen much faster than any other Parrot species because they are naturally very social creatures.

Now, you can sit by the cage and talk to your bird in a calm voice. Just place your hands on the wall of the cage for a while and sit in front of the cage quietly. The bird will approach your hand, lick it and probably even nibble at it. This is a good sign as it shows that your bird is not afraid of you. You can even move your hand around the walls and see if the bird follows your hand. If he does, then he is warming up to you.

When you are interacting with your bird, make sure that you are at his eye level at all times. When you are feeding, cleaning or even just talking to him, stay at the same level as him. If you tower over the cage, he will view you as a predator and will get scared of you. He will also assume that you mean harm if he feels like you are much larger than him in size.

Staying at eye level, on the other hand, tells him that you are part of his flock and that you are both equals in the group. This will help him trust you more and approach you more positively.

e. Bird proofing

Bird proofing is one of the most important things to do before you bring your bird home. Of course, if you do not plan to let your bird out of the cage anytime soon, it gives you more time to make your home safe for the Parrot. The moment you decide that you want to train your bird to step up or step out of the cage, it is a must to bird proof, especially if you do not plan to clip the wings of your bird.

There are a few things that you need to make sure in order to keep your home safe for a bird:

- Avoid using any Teflon pans. This may seem a little weird to you. However, the Teflon surface of a pan releases certain fumes that can be extremely dangerous for your bird. If you need to use these pans, make sure that the bird's enclosure is far away from the kitchen. It will also help if you install a really good exhaust system.
- The cage should not be placed near any hard surfaces. If your bird's wings have been clipped, he may have falls while trying to fly. A hard surface near the cage can result in broken bones and other damages to the bird.
- Do not use twine to hang toys from the roof of the cage? This can lead to entanglement, cuts and injuries. Instead, it is advised that you use metal hooks to do the same. You can also use 100% stainless steel chains for this purpose.
- The stoves should either be covered or you need to make sure that the stove has cooled down sufficiently before letting the bird out. Having a door to the kitchen may be a great idea as the bird is at a lesser risk of suffering from burns due to hot utensils, steam etc.
- Ceiling fans or table fans should always be put off before you let the bird out. If your bird is capable of flight, this is one of the most important things to do.
- Always keep the window and the entrance doors shut to prevent any chances of your bird escaping from your home. If you have large glass windows, adding plants on the sill or hanging something near the window will prevent the bird from

flying straight into it. Of course, you can also leave the windows a little dirty.

- Toilets must always be covered after you use them. If you have a pool at home, your bird should never be allowed in the area without supervision. This is simply because these birds are not great swimmers. They will drown if the accidentally fall into the pool or the toilet.

- Keep anything breakable away from the reach of the bird. If your bird is capable of flying, just put them in places where your bird is less likely to go.

With birds, you also need to be very careful while opening and shutting doors. Watch your step when the bird is out of the cage. That way, you will be able to prevent any unwanted accidents.

f. Do Quakers make good friends?

The answer to this is a definite yes. These birds make wonderful companions. But, there are some chances of risk when you force your bird to interact with children, other birds or even household pets like cats and dogs.

You need to keep your bird as happy as possible from the word go. That is when you have more success in introducing these birds to your pets or the kids in your household. Quakers thrive in homes where they feel like they are a part of the family too. If you do not include the bird in your daily routine, he will do things like scream and pluck only to get your attention. That said, Quakers are great around people but also need time on their own. If they are disturbed when they are resting or enjoying this alone time, they will get very irritated and may react negatively.

1. Quaker and other birds

That said, is it a good idea to introduce a Quaker Parrot to birds of other species. Well, owners of these birds have had varied experiences. Some birds are extremely gentle while others can be really aggressive. There are instances when the Quaker has attacked and even killed other smaller birds.

It depends a lot on the personality of your bird whether he will be a good aviary mate or not. Some Quakers will get along very easily while others may never get along with other birds. The reason for this is the nesting instinct in these birds that makes them quite different from other species of Parrots. They tend to be a lot more territorial than other species of Parrots. Now, that does not mean that one Quaker will get along with another one. It is like this, is it possible for people to get along with just about anyone? Similarly Quakers need companions that are compatible in terms of personality.

If you want to introduce a Quaker Parrot to other birds or another Quaker, it is best that you do it when the bird is young and not yet sexually mature. This is when the nesting instincts have still not kicked in. You need to make this introduction in a neutral space to ensure that there is no territorial behavior in either bird. Watch the way they react to each other when they are introduced to one another. If one bird chases or tries to attack the other, put them back in their respective cages and let them be. On the other hand, if they ignore each other and get about their own business, you can expect them to get along with one another.

If you have multiple birds at home, introduction should always be done one on one till your new bird is used to each individual bird. Then you can place him in the aviary and watch the reaction of other birds. Never force friendships between birds for their own safety. Of course, initial interactions must be supervised at all times.

2. Quaker and children

If you have a newborn baby in your home, it is advised that you do not bring home a Quaker. They both require a lot of attention. If you are unable to give the bird the attention he needs, he may grow jealous of the baby and may even attack the child.

Now, if you already have a Quaker and then have a baby, never go to the bird only after the baby is put away in the crib. Then the Quaker gets a message that he is loved only when the baby is away. That leads to jealousy and anger. Such a bird will attack the baby or may start exhibiting behavior such as feather plucking. Make sure that you go about your daily routine with the bird while the baby is in the room. It is not a good idea to let the bird out of the cage, though.

If you want to bring a Quaker home to teach your child responsibility, you must wait until the child is older. This is a good pet for pre-teens or teenagers. If you have a little one at home who is younger than 7 years of age, it is not advisable to leave him alone with the bird.

These birds have hooked beaks. That is something you must never underestimate. These beaks are strong and sharp and can inflict serious damage upon anyone. Most often birds like Quakers that are so social will be kind and gentle towards everyone in the family. But if you cross a line, he will let you know. Now with a child who is less than 7 years of age this could happen by accident, leading to serious injuries.

It is a rule of the thumb that larger Parrots are easier to form relationships with. So, if you have had a Budgie or a Cockatiel, it is not the same as having a Quaker Parrot. These birds need a lot more work to turn them into great companions. If you are patient enough, you will have a friend for life. Even if you are a first time owner or if you have a child in your home who wants a Quaker Parrot, you can both build very successful relationships with the bird if you are willing to learn and be patient with him. But a child must not be allowed to do this unsupervised.

Children tend to get scared easily and may react with a scream when the bird is being playful. In some cases, children could just get naughty and tease the bird. Both these situations are negative for your Parrot and he will react by either nipping or attacking the child. The bird is not to be blamed as he is only responding to instinct. You cannot blame the child because, well, he is a child. As an adult, you need to be very responsible about introducing your bird to the child at the appropriate age.

3. Quakers and other pets

Most pet owners are often in a dilemma whether they can bring a Parrot into a home with a pet like a cat or a dog. On one hand, you see so many online videos of birds and dogs being wonderful companions and on the other hand you cannot help but think about the instinctive behavior of these animals.

Well, instinct always wins. You see, in the wild, these animals are predators of the Quaker birds or any other bird. So, the bird may view them as a threat and initiate the attack. Now, even if the gentlest dog accidentally gets his mouth around the bird, it is certainly dangerous.

With cats, you need to be more careful as they are curious creatures. They will try to climb the cage of your bird just to figure out who this new member in the family. This curious meeting may go wrong, potentially injuring the bird and the cat. The bird is at a greater risk because the saliva of the cat is fatal to the bird.

So, before you introduce your pet to your bird, you need to weigh out all the possible interactions. However, it is certain that you need to make them aware of each other's presence. When the bird is acclimatized to your home and has settled in, you can place the cage of the bird where the dog or the cat spends most of his time.

Initially, your pet will be extremely curious and will try to sniff the cage and even be a little restless around the new creature. If the dog barks or growls, take the bird away. If the cat tries to climb on the cage, discourage that immediately.

Both behaviors are threatening for the bird and will reduce any chances of getting along in the future. Maintain these enclosed interactions until the pets do not react to the presence of your bird. The next question is whether you can let your bird out of the cage or not.

If your bird is not capable of flight, it is probably too much of a risk. In case the pet gets too excited and approaches the bird, he may not be able to get away to safety. Otherwise, you can try supervised interactions outside the cage while holding your dog or cat. If the latter gets too edgy and aggressive, you may not want to encourage these out of cage interactions.

In any case, make sure that your bird is in the cage and the pets are in their enclosure when you leave the house. They should not be able to have accidental encounters that may lead to untoward incidents. Sometimes, these unsupervised interactions may turn out to be great and sometimes, it could lead to serious injuries for both animals. The risk is too high and so, it is best that you avoid them.

Chapter 5: Caring for your Quaker

Providing adequate care is very important if you want your bird to be healthy and happy. There are some mandatory provisions that you need to make for your bird when you decide to bring one home. This chapter will tell you everything you need to know about providing proper care for your bird.

a. Housing the Quaker

You need to ensure that your bird has a safe and secure enclosure that he can spend most of his time in. It should be comfortable and clean, failing which the bird can fall seriously ill and also develop behavioral issues.

When you are housing any bird, the first thing you need to worry about is size. The cage must be bigger than the full wingspan of the bird. That means, when your bird spreads his wings in any direction, the wings must not touch the walls of the cage. Even when he flaps his wings he should not be able to touch the roof or the ceiling. In the case of a Quaker, the ideal size is 24" X 30"X 24".

The distance between the bars of the cage should not be more than $3/4^{th}$ inch. This ensures that his head or feet will not get stuck in the bars. The bars should always be wide enough for the head to pass in and out easily but not the body. Another option is to have the bars so close that your bird is just able to hold it with the beak and climb.

The next thing that you need to think about is the material. It is best that you invest in a good quality powder coated cage. Most cages may have traces of zinc or lead in them which is very harmful for the bird. A stainless steel cage is the safest option and the easiest one to maintain. The lighter the cage, the easier it is to transport. So choose the right material which is safe for the bird and easy for you to handle.

Make the cage as fun and entertaining as possible. This means, you need to add lots of toys. You can even hang some down for the bird to play with. Chewing toys, climbing toys and foraging toys are the best to keep your bird active. Of course you will need a perch that is placed at a comfortable height such that the bird has enough head space and the tail does not touch the floor either. Remember that the tail of a Quaker is long. So you need to be very careful while placing the perch. This perch should be strong and steady. If not, the bird will never climb up and will be seen only near the floor of the cage.

Choose a square or rectangular cage always as it is more spacious. Round cages restrict movement and can make your bird extremely lethargic and bored. You must also avoid suspended cages as they do not feel secure enough for the bird.

1. Essential contents of the cage
Besides toys and decorations, there are other things that are important to have inside a cage. You need to make sure that your cage has:

- **Food and water bowls:** Some cages come with a built in food and water bowl. If that is not available, you need to add them. You can get steel or porcelain ones for a decent price. These bowls are heavy and will not topple when your bird tries to play or eat. Make sure that they are shallow enough for the bird to just bend down and pick up food and water. With the water bowl, you need to make sure that there is enough head space. The thing with birds is that they tend to throw their head back to drink water. When your bird does this, he should not hurt himself.

  Feeders and bottles are a good option as well. However, they are very difficult to clean and maintain. So, it is a good idea to keep them for any travel needs. You may also need to have bottles if your bird has the habit of pooping in the water too frequently. It is necessary to have safe bowls. Make sure that there are no sharp edges that may lead to cuts on your bird's neck when he reaches in to drink or eat.

- **Substrate:** Wood shavings must always be avoided when you are making the substrate material for the cage. This is usually the material of choice when you are housing poultry. However, with birds like the Quaker Parrot, the dust can lead to a lot of sickness in the bird.

  One of the best and most preferred substrate materials is newspaper. It is easily available and is also good at absorption. Avoid glossy paper as the ink on this paper is toxic for the bird. Instead, you could use the regular matte paper. It is also very easy to change. Of course, it is also the most economic option available.

  You need to keep the bird from stepping on poop. That means you can add a bird grate to the floor and place the substrate below it. That way, the bird will not step into this and then contaminate his food and water bowls either.

  When choosing the substrate, make sure that it really absorbs well but does not retain water for too long. If it does not dry fast enough, it will become a breeding ground for bacteria and fungus that can cause life threatening illnesses in birds. Also, it should not have any toxins that the bird may accidentally come in contact with and fall ill.

  These contents of the cage are only good enough if they are maintained well. Following a religious cleaning regime is necessary to prevent any sickness in the bird. It also makes sure that your home does not have a perpetual bad odor. One thing you need to know about Parrots is that they hate to live in a mess.

2. Cage maintenance

It is mandatory that you have a daily cleaning routine for the main parts of the cage every single day. If you are not willing to do this, you must not commit to a Quaker Parrot. Here are some simple practices that will make sure that your bird has a healthy and sanitary environment.

1. What cleaning material to use?

The cleaning material that you choose should be safe for the bird and must be able to thoroughly disinfect the cage of the bird. A bird's cage is full of pathogens that you need to clean up fully.

You may use soap and water if there is any organic material that you want to remove. The solution must be very mild to prevent any irritation. Remember that soap and water does not disinfect the cage. You need to wipe the cage down with a disinfectant to make sure that it is actually free from germs and microbes.

Bleaching powder is one of the best and most easily available disinfectants. You can make a dilute solution and wipe all the contents of the cage down. Make sure that your bird is out of the cage when you do this. The fumes can irritate the bird. You can put him back after the solution has dried completely and the distinct smell is gone. If the cage is made of metal, bleaching powder may reduce its life.

An alternative is Nolvasan, which is readily available in any pet store. You could also use Virosan as it is safe for your bird. Although these products are expensive, they are very useful for the cleanliness of your bird's cage. Most of the pathogens will be eliminated with these products.

Stabilized chlorine dioxide is also a good choice to disinfect the cage. The advantage with this product is that it uses oxidation to disinfect. That makes it effective even against spores and virus. This product is also very safe. It is used to clean drinking water in many parts of Europe. There are no side effects or damages caused by the use of this product. It is also safe to clean the feeders and the water bowls with this product as it is completely safe. You just have to spray it on the surface that you want to clean and wipe it down. And, voila! Your bird's cage is free from any threats.

2. Make a schedule

The food and water containers must be cleaned on a daily basis. If you use steel or porcelain ones, they are easiest to clean. It is a good idea to keep a spare pair that you can use when the ones that you have washed are drying. Using a cleansing gel that you can get in a pet store to clean the bowl. Then, rinse it with water thoroughly. Never leave any chemical behind as it may seriously harm your bird. These bowls need to be fully dry before they are replaced.

The substrate needs to be removed and replaced on a daily basis. Most of the moisture is retained in the substrate and should be removed to prevent any fungal or bacterial growth.

Any surface that is exposed must be wiped down on a daily basis. You can use one of the disinfectants mentioned above in a very dilute form, spray it on the surface and then wipe it down after leaving it on for about 100 minutes. This is one way to make sure that your cage is sanitized and clean. In addition to that, it also increases the life of the cage.

It is a good idea to remove all the toys from the cage every fortnight and clean them thoroughly. Any severely damaged ones can be thrown away. Use a brush to remove any dry organic matter. If you notice that one of the toys is very dirty wash it immediately and dry it before replacing it. Soak the toys in a cleansing solution and rinse them completely. No chemical from the cleaning agent should be left behind as it is harmful for your bird. Then, make sure that they are fully dry before you put them back in the cage.

Make it a monthly practice to wash the cage out thoroughly. You will have to use a brush to scrub out any dry material from the floor of the cage. Using warm water makes it easier to clean the dirty parts of the cage very easily. You can simply use a soap water solution. Then, wash and rinse the cage fully. Once it is dry, spray a disinfectant and wash it down. Of course, you will have to have a stand by enclosure for your bird. Do not put the bird back until the cage is fully dry.

Some of you may want to keep the cage outdoors. Then, you must wash the whole cage twice a month. That will make sure that any pathogens that have been released into the cage by wild birds or rodents will be removed. It will also keep dust at bay.

If your bird has not been hand trained, you will need to use a towel to handle the bird. Wrap the towel around his body. Allow the ends to fall over your hands and protect them from any bites. Make sure that the head is not covered by the cloth. You can also use sturdy gloves to protect yourself from accidents.

The cage that you transfer your bird to must have a lot of food and water if this is the first time. Once the bird is trained and accustomed to this routine, it will be a lot easier for you. In case you are unsure of what cleansing agent you can use, consult your vet first. It is recommended that you check the cage thoroughly every day. In case you find any debris or peculiar droppings, clean it instantly. You definitely do not want to leave pieces of rotting food around. With Quakers, you will also have to clean out the things that they hoard in their cage as part of their nesting habits.

b. Feeding the bird

Nutrition is one aspect that you need to pay most attention to. There are several diseases that are caused solely because your bird does not receive the right food. Low nutrition also means that immunity is compromised. This results in the bird being more prone to deadly infections. Then, all your efforts to provide the bird with a clean and sanitary environment will be in vain as the bird will develop several health issues anyway.

The truth about Parrot nutrition is that the knowledge about this subject is still evolving. Several researchers across the globe reveal new requirements of the bird every time they conduct a study. What you need to make sure is that your bird is getting a good balance of the essential nutrients which includes vitamins, minerals, proteins, fats, carbohydrates and water.

The first step is to speak to your avian vet about the requirements of a Quaker Parrot. Depending upon the current health and age of your bird, he will be able to recommend the best possible options for you. You must also rely on a lot of common sense along the way to understand what will work for your bird and what will not. You have already read about the natural diet of the Quaker Parrot. You need to provide something that is close to this to keep the bird in good health.

Your bird needs a well-balanced diet that comprises of:

Seeds:

Seeds have always been the center of debate when it comes to Quaker diet. It is true that your bird's diet should never entirely comprise of seeds. However, there are seasonal seeds that are good for your bird. The commercially available bird seeds are very high in fat and low in essential nutrients. They might lead to obesity or metabolic issues in your bird.

Seed consumption must be limited. They are highly palatable and are extremely good tools for training the bird. But they should form the smallest part of your bird's diet. If your bird has been on a seed only diet at the breeder's you can get him to eat pellets by mixing the two. Then, increase the pellet portion and reduce the seeds gradually. Your bird will eventually learn to love a pellet based diet.

Pellets

These are the most essential part of your bird's diet. Pellets have several specially created formulations that ensure best nutrition for your bird. You will get special pellets to help birds through different stages of growth such as molting, sexual maturity, brooding etc. Some of them are also specially formulated to act as catalysts for certain medical treatments.

Pellets must form 75-80% of your bird's diet. So weaning the bird off is necessary. If you see sudden changes in the health of your bird when you wean him from seeds, consult your vet. He will also be able to help you with the right brand to give your bird.

Fruits and vegetables

Fresh produce should make up 20% of your bird's diet. If you give your birds vegetables that are only rich in water, the nutritional value is very low. Choose bright and pulpy fruits for the best result.

Make sure that you wash the produce well before feeding it to the bird. You can cut them into small pieces depending upon the bite size of your bird. It is recommended that you heat them up a little bit to make them more appealing to the bird. The skin can be left on usually. Quaker Parrots are very clever birds. They will pick their favorites and will refuse to eat other fruits and vegetables. Makes sure you give them a large variety of fruits and veggies to help them choose. Of course, avocado should be left out of this list as it is toxic to your bird.

It is a good idea to start the day with a bowl of pellets. Then, you can feed the fruits and vegetable to the bird after a gap of 2 to 3 hours. This will ensure that your bird will eat all the varieties of foods that you are giving him and not just his personal favorites.

Now, the thing with Parrots is that they should watch their flock eat a certain food before they eat it. So, if you want to introduce the bird to a new fruit, eat it in front of him and be very expressive about how delicious the fruit is. This will make him want to eat it too.

You must change the diet as per the stage of life your bird is in. Make sure that you consult your vet about the requirements of your bird before you make these changes. If you are giving your bird fortified pellets, supplementation is not really necessary. If your bird is tested as deficient in certain nutrients like calcium, you can give him supplements. You will get supplements that are soluble in water and also available as chew toys.

Make sure that clean water is always available for your birds. Drinking water is the only way that the nutrients that he consumes are transported throughout the body. You may offer foods from your plate as long as you know that it is good for your bird.

It is recommended that you change the pellets every day. Even if it means that you need to throw away most of the pellets from the previous day, you need to do it. Of course, fruits and veggies that are close to rotting should never be given to the bird or even left in the cage. Monitor your bird's eating habits every day. If you notice an unusual increase or decrease in the food consumed, you will have to consult your vet immediately. Also keep the food and water bowls clean. Quaker birds are very picky and will not eat or drink from a dirty dish.

b. Looking for a good avian vet

Usually, the breeder that you buy the Quaker from will be able to recommend a good avian vet. If the location is feasible and you feel like you are able to work comfortably with this vet, you can stick to him. It is a good idea to do so because the vet has all the necessary information about the bird's medical history including the vaccinations and illnesses, if any.

If the recommended vet is not feasible, you will have to look for one in the vicinity of your home. Make sure that the vet is close to your home. This will help you get to the vet easily in case of an emergency. Now, for a bird, a regular vet will not do. You need to find an avian vet. These vets have a specialized degree in treating birds and would have completed several hours of practice in facilities that provide care for birds. It is alright to take your bird to a vet who treats other pets like cats and dogs in case of an emergency. But, as far as the regular checkups are concerned, you need a specialized vet.

On an average, a vet who specializes in birds should at least see three birds everyday if he is also treating other animals like reptiles. However, if the vet is treating these many birds every month, then you need to look for more options.

The Association of Avian Vets is the best place to look for avian vets in your locality. You can log on to www.aav.org and search for the best options. Some avian vets may be registered under this organization and some may not. The ones that are registered are usually specialists in exotic birds as well. It is a great advantage if your vet is a part of the AAV as they conduct regular seminars to keep the vets updated with the latest trends in avian care.

You can also ask friends and relatives who own birds to suggest avian vets that you can take your pet to. There are several online forums and groups on social media that are exclusively for Quaker owners in your city or town. These groups will form a big part of your support system in raising your bird.

You may also talk to a regular vet and ask him or her to suggest a good avian vet in your zone. If all else fails, the best place to look is the internet or yellow pages. It is suggested that you start looking for the best options from the time you decide to bring your bird home.

Whether your avian vet has been recommended by someone or whether you have found one on your own, you need to make sure that you check out the facility before you finalize anything. Only when you pay a visit will you be able to understand whether the vet is fully equipped to care for your bird or not.

What should you look for?

There are a few standards that all good avian vets will maintain. You can look for the following things in the facility that you visit:

- **Supportive Staff:** The front office and the staff are very important as they will be your first point of contact. Observe how they talk to you when you call in to make an appointment. Are they friendly? Are they able to give you specialized instructions to transport the bird if it is a very hot or cold day?

  When you get to the vet's office, you will have to observe how they manage the birds. Are they able to handle them easily? If the birds are slightly restless and aggressive, are they afraid? Are they able to identify the common pet bird species? If you find their interaction with the birds satisfactory, it is a good sign.

- **Hygiene and facilities:** Take a tour around the facility. They should have the basic equipment like an incubator, a graham scale and temporary enclosures for the birds. The facility should be spotless. As you know already, birds are very susceptible to allergies. If you notice dust on the exposed surfaces or dampness in the cage or hospital enclosure, it means that they are not taking good care of their space. That puts your bird at the risk of contracting additional infections and diseases at the vet's clinic.

- **Checkup Practices:** Carefully watch the way the vet examines the bird. If the examination is done while the bird is in the cage, it may not be good enough. Ask why the examination was done without taking the bird out. Normally, the bird must be taken out of the cage for a thorough examination of the feathers, the bones, the beak and the feet to rule out any infections and diseases.

The duration of the examination is also very important. It normally takes about 30 minutes to check a bird thoroughly. Some doctors will shorten this duration to 10 minutes to be able to have more patients per day. That is a sign of negligence that you need to worry about.

- **Emergency facilities:** Your vet needs to be available to you 24/7. If not he should at least have a tie up with a facility that can attend to your bird at any time in case of an emergency. It is also a good idea if your vet has a pet hospital that your bird can be admitted in if he needs special care or in case of a surgery etc. They should have access to such facilities if they do not have it in their own clinic.
- **Keeping up with trends:** Your vet needs to stay updated with all the current practices of bird care. This means that he should subscribe to magazines, attend seminars or even be part of avian vet groups to stay in the loop. Only if he is

interested in improving standards of care is your bird definitely safe under his care.

1. Is Insurance necessary?

In the case of pet birds, the insurance options are very limited. However, it is a good idea to have a plan for your bird, as avian healthcare can get a little expensive. The issue with pet insurance for birds is that several costs are usually not covered under them. Unlike a dog or a cat insurance that pays for practically everything related to pet healthcare, there is not such a perfect insurance plan for birds. This is probably because of the lifespan of the bird. A Quaker Parrot will live for up to 30 years. So, the insurance coverage is limited.

The two best insurance options that are recommended by most bird owners are Pet Assure and Veterinary Pet insurance. These policies will offer the following coverage for your bird:

- **Veterinary costs:** They provide coverage for emergency care and also some diagnostic processes. You may also be able to get coverage for a portion of the consultation fee that you pay to your vet. But, as mentioned before, veterinary costs available annually are limited, given the long life of the birds. You should be able to get annual coverage of up to $1500 or £750.

- **Third part liability:** In case any damage is caused to another person or someone else's property because of your bird, a part of it is covered by your insurance plan.

- **Overseas cover:** This policy covers any costs incurred when you travel overseas with your bird. This includes medical care that is required by a bird who has just undergone the stress of traveling.

- **Loss or Death cover:** This feature is available if you have a rare species or sub species of the Quaker Parrot in your home. You will have to check with your insurance provider about the conditions related to this cover. You will have to invest in a good quality cage and make other security arrangements in order to get this cover.

Depending upon the type of coverage that you choose, your insurance premium can go up to about $250 or £150. In case you have multiple birds at home, you will get a discount on this premium as well. Usually, you can get up to 10% off on each bird.

The difference with Veterinary Pet Insurance or Pet Assure is that the former allows you to choose the vet that you want to get your bird checked by. However, they do not cover certain diagnostic procedures. In the case of Pet Assure, coverage is better but the Vet that you choose must belong to their network to get any coverage.

In any case, it is always a good idea to open up an emergency fund for your Quaker Parrot. Some owners do not get any cover and just put away the premium in a separate account. That can work too if you can be consistent with these funds. An insurance is great for your bird just to make sure that if you use these funds for a family emergency, you have something to fall back upon.

Chapter 6: Bonding with Quaker Parrots

For all Parrots, bonding with one person or one mate is very important to feel a sense of security. You will only be able to play with your bird and actually enjoy his intelligent ways when you have bonded with him and gained his trust completely. This requires a lot of patience and time on your part. With Quaker Parrots, the advantage is that although they may be close to one family member or their cage mate, they will also bond with the rest of their family. This is because of their natural instinct to live in a community.

a. Bonding or Over-bonding?

Yes, there is such a thing as over bonding which is actually the root cause of several behavioral problems. Proper training prevents over bonding and ensures that you have a well behave bird who is friendly and easy to handle.

What are the signs of bonding?

From the time you bring the bird into your home, you will notice that he slowly warms up to you and your family. Then, the bonding process progresses to a point when you are able to keep your bird on your shoulder and go about your daily activities. Let us take a look at the signs that show you that your bird is bonding with you.

Warming up: The Initial Stage

Your Parrot will stop other activity and watch you when you are in the room or when you are passing by the cage. He will not be scared or nervous, however.

He will follow your movements and will respond to your talking with different vocalizations. In the case of the Quaker, he may just repeat the words that you say.

The bird moves towards you when you approach the cage.

When you offer food from your hand, the bird eats it calmly.

The Progression: After the bird is "Hand tamed"
He will step up on to your finger and will also let you pet him.
He will call out to you when you are not around and he misses you.
He may climb on your hand or shoulder, even when you do not ask him to.

The bond: Your bird loves you
He will preen and groom your hair. Even if that means he is just making it messier.
He will not resist grooming activities like bathing or wing clipping. He will even let you hold him in awkward positions such as being upside down.
He begins to trust you completely and even displays mating behavior such as regurgitation of food when you are around.

Signs of over-bonding

The bird becomes very angry and aggressive when you talk to anyone else, especially another bird. He will scream and will even tear his toys apart.
He is only happy if you are around and will always groom your hair or will try to feed you and display courting behavior. When you are gone, he will scream, become very scared or will just be depressed.
The bird will not allow anyone else to handle him or touch him except the person he has bonded with.
If any other person receives a slight bit of attention from the one he has bonded with, he will attack and bite them.
The bird is extremely defensive about the person he has bonded with. If anyone tries to even touch the human he has bonded with, he will bite them. He will also attack other pets around your home.
He will not let anyone else feed him.

Having an over-bonded Parrot can be very difficult. You will not be able to travel and leave the bird in someone else's care. He is also a potential threat to everyone around your home, especially children. The only way to prevent over-bonding is properly training your bird and socializing him. This is not a difficult thing to do with Quaker Parrots.

b. Training your bird

Training a Quaker can take a few days or even a few months depending upon the personality of your bird. The most important thing to do is to build trust and tell the bird that you mean no harm.

1. Building trust

The first thing you want to accomplish with your bird is trust. This is a slow process but once you have managed it, it can be extremely rewarding. Start by just spending a few minutes every day, talking to the bird and just placing your hand on the walls of the enclosure.

If you are the one feeding him every day, he is likely to bond faster. If your bird begins to respond by approaching your hand, licking it or nibbling at it slowly, it is a good sign. You can then start offering treats through the bars of the cage. If your bird does not eat it, just leave it in the cage and keep trying. Once the bird accepts a treat from your hand, the next step is to let him out of the cage.

Just open the cage door and let the bird come out. He will probably climb up on the cage and just explore the space around. Make sure that the space is safe for your bird and free from threats like pets or ceiling fans.

Then, you can hold out some treats in your hand and see if the bird will approach your hand. When your bird starts eating comfortably from your hand, it means that he is tamed enough to start the actual training.

Putting the bird back is easy. Just leave a few of his favorite treats or toys in the cage and he will go to them. In case your bird is reluctant to go into the cage before he is hand tamed, use toweling to handle him. Wrap his body with a thick towel and let the ends fall over your hand. Then, pick him up gently holding the wings down and put him back in the cage. Treats and toys will help him understand that the cage is a fun place to be in.

2. Step up training

When a bird is ready to step up on your finger or hand, it means that he trusts you completely. Now, step up is more than a trust building command. Your bird must be able to step up in case of any emergency. If there is a natural calamity or if the bird is in danger and is unable to fly, stepping up will really help him get out of a dangerous situation.

You can begin the step up training with target training. Use a stick with a treat on the end and hold it through the cage, close to the bird. He may bite at it immediately. If not, gently touch the bird's beak with the stick. This stick is called the target. Once the bird understands that every time you present the target, he is going to get a treat, he will begin to look forward to it. He will even bite at it when there is no treat at the end.

Slowly start moving this target along the cage walls. If your bird follows it, it means that he is target trained. Now, open the door of the cage and hold the target there. The bird will start to come out of the cage following the target. When he does this, give him a treat. Do this a couple of times until he knows that getting out of the threat calls for a treat.

Then hold your finger horizontally in front of the cage and the target just behind the finger. When the bird is out of the cage, say "step up" and hold the finger steady. The bird may nibble at your finger as a way to make sure that it is safe to climb up. Do not withdraw the finger or move it as the bird will lose trust. If the bird does step up, praise him abundantly and give him a treat. Slowly the bird will step up even without the target or the treat.

This is when he is fully bonded with you and trusts you completely.

You can later encourage him to step on your shoulder or your head using the same technique. Once the bird is ready to step up on your shoulder, you can include him in all your daily activities and make the bond stronger.

Putting the bird back in the cage might become challenging. This is because he views this as an unpleasant experience as he will have to go away from you. So, place his favorite treats and toys in the cage after putting him back as an indication of the fun times ahead. Then, the bird will learn to stay by himself and keep himself entertained when put back in the cage. If not, he may develop separation anxiety and scream whenever you go away.

3. Toilet training

When you are taking your bird all over the house with you after step up training, the last thing you want is your furniture and carpet to be covered with poop. You need to tell your bird that he can poop only in an assigned place and not anywhere else in the house. The first step is to help him understand that his cage is a good place to do his business.

You can start doing this with the first poop of the day. In the morning, when you are feeding the bird and cleaning up the bowls, place a fresh newspaper under the perch and wait for the bird to poop. Watch his body language when he does this. Knowing the changes in the body is very useful in further training. When he poops praise him and give him a treat. That tells him that pooping in the cage is a good thing.

Usually, when birds poop, they tend to crunch their bodies and hold it stiff. Other birds may have other changes in the body language. When you begin to step the bird up and walk around your home with him, watch out for these signs. The moment you see this you can put a tissue under the bird and let him go about his business. When he does poop on the paper, praise him. If he poops elsewhere don't react. No reaction is worse than reprimanding for a bird.

He will eventually learn that pooping on paper is good. You can then step the training up and hold the paper over a bin or inside the cage. When the bird uses this designated place, praise him and give him a treat. He will slowly understand that every time he needs to poop, he will have to go to the bin or to the cage in order to keep you happy.

Birds as large as the Quaker will poop every 20 minutes at least. This means that there are chances of accidents. Be patient and do not reprimand the bird unnecessarily. Instead, until your bird is fully potty trained, keep the expensive carpets and rugs away.

4. Behavior training

There are two most common behavioral problems with birds that you need to address. This is especially true for a Quaker Parrot. They tend to be too loud and can get a little aggressive and bite. Both these behaviors are usually to get your attention. If you give your bird that, he will continue this behavior for a long time to come.

Curbing screaming

Quaker birds may scream at a certain time of the day. This is acceptable as it is their natural urge to call out to their flock at a certain time of the day. If your Parrot, on the other hand, screams every time you leave the room, you have a problem on hand. You need to make sure that the bird understands that screaming is not the best way to get your attention.

You can do this by ignoring the bird when he screams and giving him attention only when he stops screaming. If you come running back to the room when you hear the bird scream he gets a message that this is what he needs to do in order to get your attention. If you come in and scold him in a loud voice, it is worse. He will think that you are responding to his calls. Instead, come in only when he stops shouting. That tells him that you will be close to him only when he behaves in an appropriate manner.

Whenever you leave the room, it is a good idea to put a few toys into your bird's cage whenever you leave the room. This teaches the bird that it is time for some fun when you are going out. He will become more independent that way and will stop screaming everytime you left the room for even just a minute.

Curbing biting

When a bird bites you, the natural reaction is to shout or loudly say "No!" Well, that is precisely what your bird wants- your attention. So, when your bird bites you, as painful as it may be, do not react.

Instead, gently press his head down. Birds hate being in such an uncomfortable position. If he is perched on your finger or shoulder, just move it a little when he bites you. For birds, losing balance from a perch is a very unpleasant thing. Of course, you can use this method called "earthquake" method only after you have completed step up training fully.

The last thing to do would be to put him back in the cage. A bird bites to seek attention and when you do the opposite and put him away, he immediately realizes that you do not like it. Eventually he will understand that you are only going to be with him when he is well behaved.

5. Training tips
It is possible to speed up the process of training your bird if it is consistent. Here are some tips that will help you train the bird better:

- ✓ Set a routine: The training process must happen at a given time of the day, on a daily basis. Even if it is just for fifteen minutes, you need to do it.
- ✓ Don't confuse the bird: If you are using a certain stick as a target, use the same stick every day. Don't change it every day. The commands and gestures that you use should be consistent. If you say "step up" one day and "come on up" the other, the bird may get confused.

✓ Do not reprimand: If your bird doesn't perform a certain trick, don't be impatient. Even when he fails be kind and approving. The only way to make training stimulating for the bird is to keep praising him abundantly.

With the target training method, you can teach your Parrot to pick cards, shake hands and even complete obstacle races. The idea is to just keep repeating the same thing over and over and treating the bird every time he performs the task you want him to.

c. The talking Quaker

You can never talk about a Quaker Parrot and leave out the talking bit. They are the most talkative birds and are the best at picking up words and phrases. In fact, it almost seems like these birds understand what they are saying as it is always on point in terms of the context. But how do you get your bird to talk and say the words that you want him to?

First, you Quaker may pick up certain words on his own. If you say "Hello" or "Hi" every morning when you feed the bird, he will respond with the same words. If he hears a certain word or phrase over and over again, he is most likely to say it. So, watch what you say around your Quaker. It is almost as good as having a child around who is learning to speak. You do not want him to learn any cuss words. So be very careful about what you say when the Quaker is in the room. Sometimes, it could just be extremely embarrassing for you when he says something blasphemous in front of your guests.

Now, if you want to teach a Quaker a specific word or phrase, you can do it by saying it over and over to him at a certain time of the day. Let us say you want to teach him to sing "Happy Birthday". You will have to find a time, maybe when you finish work or just before you leave for work. Sing one line of the song every day to him a couple of times. He will recite it back to you sooner or later. You can give a cue to him such as "Let's sing Happy Birthday" and then sing the song out. Sing one line at a time. When he picks up a full line, reward him and repeat it till he recites it easily. Then you can move on to the next few lines. Make sure you sing the lines he knows first and then the new lines so that he learns them in order.

You will see that the Quaker spends a lot of time mumbling to himself. This is only him practicing the lines that he is learning. Other things that can help is playing the song you want him to learn on a DVD or on the TV. If you let your birds watch cartoons for 20 minutes a day, he is going to pick up a vast vocabulary before you know it.

Here are some songs that many Quaker owners have taught their birds successfully:

The nursery rhyme *Bingo*
You are my sunshine
How much is that doggie in the window By Pattie Page
The nursery rhyme *I am a teapot.*

You can teach your Quaker Parrot a host of different songs. Songs with repetitive and easy lyrics are the best ones for your bird.

d. Quaker body language

One common body language you will notice with a Quaker is constant head bobbing and shaking. This normally does not mean anything and is just a natural thing for the bird. However, there are some specific movements and postures of the bird that you need to watch in order to understand what he is communicating with you. This is one of the most important things you need to know if you want to form a strong bond with your bird.

Flashing the pupils: Parrots can control their pupils. If they dilate it, it is an indication of pleasure, anger or nervousness. You need to examine the surroundings of the bird to understand what this "pinning" or "flashing" signifies.

Tongue clicking: This is a sign of pleasure and is often an invitation to you to come and play with him.

Beak clicking: A sharp clicking sound made from the beak shows that your bird is feeling threatened. There could be some object or person in the room that the bird is scared of. He will additionally raise a foot and also extend his neck almost as if he is defending the cage.

Beak grinding: You well hear the bird grinding his beak at night mostly. This is a sign of satisfaction and security.

Beak wiping: When the bird is in an aviary, this is a sign of defense against the other birds or a warning sign. If your bird is alone and displaying this behavior, he is trying to get something out of his beak.

Regurgitation: This behavior is displayed before their mates. Usually, a bird will regurgitate food and feed the contents to its partner. This is just what he is trying to do if he has a strong bond with you.

Head shaking: If your bird moves the head from side to side almost like he is dancing or waving the head, he is trying to get your attention. The bird will even tilt his head to one side and look at you as a sign of interest towards what you are doing.

Lowering the head: The bird will pull his wings close and lower the head and will almost look like he is about to fly. This is his way of telling you that he wants to come to you.

Beak fencing: This is only seen when there are multiple birds in the cage. The birds will hold each other's beak almost like they are jousting. It is considered to be some sort of sexual behavior.

Panting: If your bird is overheated or is too exhausted, then panting is observed. It is basically a sign of discomfort.

Wing drooping: This is normal in young birds. If your bird is an adult, then it is a sign of illness.

Wing flipping: A sharp flip or flick of the wing shows displeasure. It could also mean that your bird is just trying to set his feathers in place.

Quivering: If the body or wings quiver, it is a sign of distrust. Talk to such a bird in a calm and comforting voice.

Marching: if the bird marches with his head down, he is being defensive or aggressive. On the other hand if his head is up, he is inviting you to play with him.

Tail bobbing: This is usually a sign of sickness or fatigue, especially when the tail bobs when your bird is breathing.

Tail wagging: When the bird sees his favorite person or toy, he wags his tail as a sign of happiness.

Tail fanning: This is a dominant or aggressive behavior that basically tells you to back off.

Barking: The bird is not mimicking another pet in your home. This is a natural vocalization that that is meant to show dominance.

Purring: If the bird's body is relaxed when he is purring, it shows contentment. However, if the body is still and the pupils are dilated, it is a sign of aggression.

Whistling, Talking and Singing: These vocalizations tell you that your bird feels secure and safe. These are signs of a very happy bird.

Chattering: You will hear the bird chattering or mumbling. He is only making his presence felt and is trying to get your attention.

e. Keeping a Quaker entertained

Mental stimulation is one of the most important things for a Quaker Parrot. You will have to spend a lot of time with the bird to make sure that he is entertained and happy. If not, you will soon notice behavioral issues like feather plucking which is a result of boredom. But, it is not possible for you to eternally be around your bird. So, the question is how do you keep him entertained while you are going about your routine?

Toys are your first choice when it comes to entertaining a Quaker. There are a variety of toys such as chewing toys, climbing toys and foraging toys that you can give your Quaker. But, the only problem is that your Quaker will get bored with toys very easily. So, you can come up with innovative and economical options like hiding seeds in paper and letting your bird forage through it. The more toys you give your bird, the more entertained he is going to be.

You can even buy special birdie DVDs that you can play. These DVDs will also help the bird learn new words. If you are in the living room reading or watching the television, you can keep your bird in a play pen near you. That way he will also be able to observe you, look around and stay entertained.

Placing many tiny food dishes around the cage will force your bird to move around and eat. Covering these dishes with cotton or paper will also make it a fun foraging activity for the bird. Of course, it is added work for you because you will have to clean more dishes.

All you need to do for your bird is provide him with a lot of new experiences. The more he is engaged in activities around the house, the more likely he is to be chirpy and cheerful. Once he learns to perch on your shoulder, you can even include him in safe household chores such as folding laundry. He will also feel like he is close to you for longer. In case of Quaker Parrots, you can also let him interact with other people in the family or even your friends. They are usually open to these experiences and will be playful.

f. Grooming

Grooming is one of the most essential parts of bird care. Normally, they groom themselves by preening their feathers and tucking them into place. They will use the water from their bowls to wet their feathers and keep them clean. There is a certain gland called the uropygial gland that secretes an oil which helps keep your bird's feathers water proof. The bird will pick this oil up with his beak and smooth it over his feathers. However, there are some grooming activities that you need to engage your bird in. This is also a great bonding activity for you and your bird.

1. Bathing

Parrots require regular bathing in order to stay healthy. They may even take a dip in their water bowl once in a while to keep themselves cool. But, you need to make it a point to give your bird a bath every 15 days in order to keep his feathers clean and free from any matting.

You need not use any soap on your bird unless there is any debris or dirt on the feathers. It is a good idea to consult your vet before using a certain soap on your bird. Some of them may have chemicals that are toxic for your bird. Use soap locally on the area that is dirty and rinse it gently with warm water.

The best way to bathe your bird is to mist his feathers. If he enjoys it, he will lift his feathers and move around allowing you to continue. On the other hand, if he begins to crouch or back away, it means that he does not like it. Never spray directly on the bird's face.

You can also use a shallow water bath to let your bird take a dip. Let the bird step up on your finger. Then lower your hand till the bird just touches the water a little. If your bird wants to take a bath, he will hop in. If you want to urge him to take a bath, you can also put some spinach leaves in the water. The bird will hop in and chew on the seeds while taking a bath.

Some people also place a perch under the shower to mimic rainfall and let the bird take a bath. It is not a good idea for a

Quaker because they originate in areas with very little rainfall. The shower can be upsetting for you bird.

2. Wing Clipping

It is never advisable for first time owners to clip the wings of the bird themselves. You must make sure that you consult your vet and learn how to do this before you try it on your bird. If not, two things can happen- you could cut a blood feather, causing profuse bleeding. Or you could clip the wings unevenly. Your bird relies on his wings to get his balance. If they are not clipped properly, he will try to even them out himself, plucking the feathers out in the process. If this becomes a habit, it will turn into a behavioral problem.

If you want to clip the wings at home, you need to only cut out the first three primary feathers. These are the first three longest feathers on the wing. Pick your bird up using a towel. Now, hold him on your thigh face down. Wrap him in the towel, exposing only the wing that is to be clipped and, of course his head. Spread the feathers out and cut out 1 cm from each of the three primary feathers. Do the same on the other side. Then, open out both the wings and examine them to be sure that they are even.

If you cut a blood feather accidentally, stop the bleeding immediately using a styptic pencil or cornstarch. Then, hold it down with a piece of clean gauze.

3. Beak and toe trimming

This grooming process is optional. If you notice that your bird's toes and beak are getting stuck in the toys or any fabric, you can trim it to avoid any accidents. If the beak or toe of your bird is stuck to the fabric on your sofa and he tries to move suddenly, there are chances that the whole toe rips off or the beak is severely damaged. To avoid this, trim the sharp ends.

Wrap the bird with a towel, only exposing the part that you want to trim. With of the beak, gently lift the upper mandible with your finger and feel the sharp end. Keep the beak supported and trim the beak using a nail file. When you feel that it is just blunt, stop trimming. If the nail or the toe is too short, the bird will be unable to climb and hold properly.

Even with the toe, make sure that you have a finger supporting the nail you want to trim to avoid any chances of breakage or unwanted damage.

Remember that bonding with a bird as intelligent as the Quaker requires a lot of effort from your end. These birds will analyze every situation that they are put into and even the slightest doubt will break their trust. If you have adopted a bird that has been abused, this will take a longer time. You will also need a lot of assistance from your avian vet to gain the trust of such birds. Take it one step at a time and make sure that you do not rush him.

Chapter 7: Breeding Quakers

If your bird is adopted, make sure that you check the conditions pertaining to breeding your bird. In any case, your bird will instinctively feel the urge to breed when he is about 1-2 years old. If he thinks of you as the mate, he will perform breeding rituals like regurgitation. Females may become hormonal and will also become quite territorial during the breeding season. Quaker Parrots breed in the warmer months. If you decide to breed your birds, you need to make sure that you provide all the necessary conditions for the birds to breed successfully and also raise healthy baby birds.

a. Introducing birds

If you know from the beginning that you want to breed your Quaker Parrots, it is a good idea to start with a pair of babies. That way, they will bond with one another as they grow and will be compatible. You also need to make sure that you have one male and one female bird. Since Quaker Parrots of the opposite gender look the same, sexing needs to be done surgically or through DNA analysis.

If you want to introduce a mate to your bird in the breeding season, it is a little more challenging. You will have to follow a 30 day quarantine period before you introduce the birds to one another. It is better to introduce the birds in a neutral area. If you put the new bird into the cage of the current bird, the latter will be more territorial and vice versa. Usually females tend to be more aggressive in the case of Quaker Parrots.

Watch them when you introduce them. If they go about their business and do not get edgy, they may be compatible. If there is any aggression, put the birds in the same room but different cages and allow them to socialize. It is mandatory for the two cages to be identical. One must never be bigger than the other if you want them to think of each other as equals and socialize.

When the birds begin to show some interest in one another, you can put them in a cage together. Having a separate breeding cage is a good idea. If not, put the aggressive bird into the cage of the non-aggressive one and not the other way around. This way dominant behavior can be curbed.

Allow the birds to spend time with one another. If you see that they begin to preen each other or feed each other, they are a compatible pair. If not, try to socialize them by letting them interact on neutral grounds first.

b. Setting the nesting box

Once you have a compatible pair, you can set up a nesting box during the breeding season. It is a good idea to put this box outside the cage. If you have pets at home, you will have to put the birds away in a separate room that remains closed. The box is typically wide and deep. This gives the birds room to move around. A deep box mean that the birds will not take the nesting material out. With Quaker birds, they will exhibit nesting behavior and will try to hoard all thread like items in this box in an attempt to build a nest.

It is best to get a box that is made of wood. Wood helps the birds stay warm, as opposed to metal that can get cold. When the incubation period arrives, wood also retains moisture. The advantage with metal ones is that they last longer and are easier to clean. Make sure that the nesting box is secured tightly.

The opening for this box should be on top. If you provide a wooden nesting box, your Quaker birds will chew them and modify them a little. Having a trap door at $1/3^{rd}$ the height of the box allows you to access the nesting box to feed the birds or remove the babies when the time comes. To help the birds climb in and out of the box, add a wire mesh strip from the top of the box to the bottom. This acts as a ladder.

You can fill the nesting box almost all the way up to the opening with pine shavings. You can also use shredded newspaper. The birds will take out all the unwanted nesting material.

c. Diet

You need to give your bird a good diet to stay healthy during the breeding season. The female may require calcium supplements to ensure that the egg shells are intact. In case your bird is still not on a full pellet diet, this is not the time to wean him. You will give the bird the regular diet to prevent any stress. You can just add vitamin mineral supplements to their diet and even give them a cuttlebone to chew on.

If your bird is already on a pellet diet with fresh produce, you only have to worry about giving them the pellets recommended for the breeding period. No added supplementation is necessary with pellets as they are already fortified. You can place a cuttlebone just in case and the bird will chew on it if she needs the calcium.

d. Egg laying

After about 25 hours of the fertilization of the egg, the female will lay the first egg. She will lay about 4-8 eggs, laying one each day. She will have a second clutch of eggs after a month. If you want the bird not to lay the second clutch you can reduce day time to about 10 hours. You can move the birds to a dark room or could just turn the light off early. Just when the bird is about to lay the first egg, her droppings become smelly and large. She will also show evident abdominal distension.

If you see that the hen is leaving the eggs dormant without sitting on them, you will have to increase the temperature of the nest using an aquarium heater. Parrots are known for abandoning their clutch. If you see that your bird does not sit on the eggs and incubate them even after increasing the temperature, you will have to incubate the eggs artificially.

If the hen does brood, the incubation period is about 26 days.

e. Hand feeding the birds

You will have two options to choose from once the babies have hatched. You may allow the parents to feed and raise the babies in which case the birds are more social towards other birds. The other option is to hand feed the birds and make them tame. The former are better breeders while the latter make better pets. So it really depends upon what you plan to do with the hatchlings.

If you decide to hand feed the birds, the ideal age to remove them from the cage is when they are about 3-4 weeks old. This is when the birds are in their pin feather stage. Their feathers look like quills at this stage. This is the best age as the birds are able to hold the body heat and will not require any artificial heat. These birds also have the advantage of being raised by their parents and will be healthier. Immunity is better as the parents will pass on antibodies while feeding the babies.

Choose a formula recommended by your vet. Prepare the formula as per the instructions on the package. You need to make sure that the formula is heated to about 100 degrees F and not more than that. This can scald the insides of the delicate baby bird.

It is better to use a spoon to feed the baby as opposed to a syringe as you will be able to control the food going into the belly of the baby. That way you reduce the risk of choking the baby. Feeding with a spoon is much slower. So chances of overfeeding are fewer. When the baby is full, you will be able to see the signs that will tell you when to stop feeding. You will also spend more time with the baby when you feed him with a spoon.

In case you pull the babies out of the nest earlier or have to hand feed them at an earlier stage because they were artificially incubated, you will have to purchase a brooder that will keep the babies warm as you feed them. The formula must be made very watery and should be given to the bird in small quantities. Then you wait for the crop to empty and feed the baby again. At a very young age, you may have to feed the baby every two hours.

In the pinfeather stage, you can feed the baby 4-5 times and give him some time to rest overnight. That way the crop will be fully empty and he will be ready for next meal.

f. Weaning

During the hand feeding period, you will have to keep the birds in warm boxes or bins. When they are ready to be weaned, they are also ready for the cages. Until then, they are too small for a cage.

You know that the bird is ready to be weaned when he starts handling small objects with his beak or tries to climb using the beak. You will now reduce the formula to twice a day and introduce the bird to eating on his own. Weaning basically means that you are getting the bird to a stage when he can eat on his own without your help or the parent's help.

Place the babies in a cage that is lined with newspaper. Place a feeding bowl and a water bowl. You need one for each chick and it should be shallow enough for the bird to eat from. It is recommended that you put the bird into this cage after hand feeding in the morning. If the birds are very hungry, they may refuse to eat on their own.

You will be able to attract the babies to the new food, preferably special baby pellets, by mixing in rice crispies. You will see that they do not mind experimenting as long as their tummy isn't fully empty. Eventually they will stop eating in the evening. Then they will slowly take to eating on their own and will wean with time. Never rush the baby. Prepare a feeding routine and stick to and they will eventually learn to eat all their food on their own.

Chapter 8: Travelling with your Quaker

Vehicles and birds are not always the best match. If you want to travel with your Quaker, you will have to introduce him to your car first and then take him on drives. This is a very different experience for the bird and can often lead to a lot of stress and anxiety. The next challenge is to travel overseas. There are so many restrictions with respect to traveling internationally with birds that you will have to take several precautions. This chapter will help you figure out your bird's travel needs and make the process easier.

a. Quakers and cars

Getting your bird introduced to a car is a step by step process. It can demand a lot of patience from your end or it could be very easy to get your bird to love drives. It depends upon the personality of the bird and the measures you take to make this a positive experience for your bird.

- Step 1: Get the bird used to the car. Just transfer him to a smaller travelling cage and place the cage in the car. Make sure that the air conditioner is on. It is not advisable to leave windows open when you are travelling with birds as they may be stressed by drafts. If he shows discomfort take him home. Try this till the bird is used to the car and remains calm inside.

- Step 2: Take short drives around the block. Give the bird plenty of water and food to keep him calm. Of course, water should be given through a bottle to prevent any spilling on the way. Make sure that the cage is lined with lots of substrate. You can also give your bird a toy to stay calm. Then drive slowly and keep talking to the bird. He may be scared and may retreat in one corner of the cage. It is alright. Keep the drive short and take him home. Do this till the bird is calm during these short trips.

- Step 3: Now your bird is ready for a long drive. Prepare the cage with food, water and substrate. If you have any bags to take with you, introduce these bags during the short rides so that the bird can get used to the colors and the shapes. Take breaks every half an hour to make sure that your bird is not stressed.

b. Going overseas

If you have to travel overseas or move permanently, you will have to really think about it when you have a bird. If it is temporary, you may not want to stress the bird. It is best to leave your bird under someone else's care while you are away. However, if you have to move, you need to be sure that your bird is allowed in the state or country that you plan to move to. If he is not allowed there, you will have to either switch your moving plans or find him a foster home. The latter is very stressful for the bird. You see, having a Quaker is like having a baby. Make him your top priority always. Unless you do not have an option, it is not a kind thing to do to give your bird up. Before you travel overseas with your bird, here are a few things you need to do:

- Check with the Fish and Wildlife department of the place that you are traveling to about the restrictions with respect to Quakers. Some countries and states, like Georgia, do not allow you to have these birds as pets. Others require you to obtain a permit or a license to bring your bird to their country.
- You can contact your local Wildlife Department to check about the procedure to obtain a permit. Usually, you will be able to get a permit within 60 days of application to the concerned authority.
- Once the permit is in place, you need to find an airline that has facilities to help you transport your bird safely. Read all the safety guidelines and provisions about livestock transport. Only when you are convinced should you opt for a certain airlines. Make sure that all the transits are in the same airlines to prevent any sudden changes in the rules and regulations.

- Obtain a travelling cage as per the guidelines. Prepare the cage with water, food and substrate. For long flights, the airlines will provide feeding services for your bird. Keeping him harnessed is a good idea to keep him safe.
- Having the wings clipped is a great option as it will prevent any drama during the customs and security checks. The bird is easier to handle and the chances of escaping are lower when his wings have been clipped.
- Upon reaching your destination, have your bird examined by the vet. He may have symptoms of stress such as vomiting and dizziness because of the flight and the change in altitude. Immediate examination will makes sure that he is safe.
- When you reach your new home, leave the bird in a quiet room with fresh water and food. Let him calm down and follow the same housebreaking procedure as mentioned above.

c. Getting a sitter

If you plan to travel while you leave your bird behind, the best thing to do would be to look for a friend or relative that you trust to keep your bird. In case they are unavailable, check for hostel facilities at your Vet's. If that is not available or if your vet's hostel is not satisfactory, you can look for a sitter who will come home and take care of your bird while you are away.

You can look up the National Association of Professional Pet Sitters website to find good sitters in your vicinity. Make sure that you interview the sitter before finalizing on one. You need to look for a sitter who is:

- Comfortable handling birds and preferably has one of his own.
- Equipped to provide first aid to your bird if necessary.
- Willing to provide a substitute in case he or she is unable to attend to your bird for some reason.
- Able to manage medical emergencies or has the contacts to assure you that help reaches your bird.
- Insured for third party liability in case something untoward were to happen to your bird.

Once you have finalized upon the pet sitter, give him or her all the details about your Quakers feeding routine and also his general routine. Make sure you have the sitter's alternate contact number. You must also leave your contact number, the vet's number and an emergency contact number with the sitter.

It can be hard for you to leave your bird under a stranger's care. You could ask your pet sitter to come over and take care of the bird for a few days while you are still around. That is a great bonding exercise and it also allows you to figure out whether the sitter is really trustworthy or not. Knowing that your bird is in good hands allows you to travel without any worries. You can also ask a neighbor or friend to check in on the bird every now and then. Be sure to call your sitter at least once each day when you are away.

Chapter 9: Quaker Parrot Health

Quaker Parrots are very hardy birds that are known to handle any sort of stress better than most other Parrots. However, even these birds are prone to several health conditions that may deteriorate their health by the day and, in worst cases, even be fatal for the bird. The important thing that you need to know as the owner of the bird is to identify any form of illness in your bird and ensure that you take preventive measures to ensure that none of the diagnosed conditions recur in your precious bird.

a. Is your bird unwell?

The first step towards good pet healthcare is being able to understand that your bird is unwell. Most diseases will occur with symptoms that are easy to notice. This will help you provide necessary healthcare in the early stage of the process. That way, you are ensuring that treatment is more successful and recovery is also faster in your bird. Here are some signs that you need to look out for:

A sudden change in the attitude of your bird is the first step towards understanding that something is wrong. A bird that is healthy is generally very aware of their surroundings. They will also engage in playing more actively. The posture of the bird is upright and the weight is always equally distributed between the two legs. A healthy bird has great balance and is extremely steady. The wings are held close to the body and the bird seems relaxed at all times. If your bird is healthy, he will be able to recover from stress faster, too. But, if your bird is unwell, here are a few signs that you will definitely see:

- The bird is unable to balance himself.
- He will spend most of his time on the floor of the cage.
- He may become aggressive suddenly.
- The head is always tucked in between the wings.
- His food and water consumption will reduce drastically.

- Even if they are eating normally, the rate of dropping increases, making nutrients unavailable to the body.
- The bird suddenly loses more than 10% of the body weight.
- You will see that the bird is unable to breathe properly. Breathing is very difficult or labored.
- Tail bobbing is seen when the bird tries to breathe.
- Open mouth breathing occurs even when the bird has not participated in any physically draining activity.
- The respiratory rate does not return to normal for a long time after play.
- Redness and swelling is seen in the area around the ears.
- Overgrowth of the beak is a definite sign of malnutrition or any metabolic disease.
- Discharge or masses are seen near the oral cavity. This part of bird should have a light pink color to signify health.
- The papillae or projections around the cloaca are not pointed and sharp as they ought to be.
- The keel does not have proper muscle definition and the bird seems underweight.
- If you feel like the keel area is not palpable, it shows that the bird is overweight.
- The skin of your bird should be free from any redness or peculiar coloration.
- If you see sudden bald patches on the body of the bird when he is not molting, it is an indication of some health issue.
- If the shape of the feather becomes abnormal, it shows that the bird may have some sort of viral infection.
- If your bird develops a skin abnormality, this could even escalate to feather plucking issues.
- The vent of your bird or the cloaca should be clean always. If there is any fecal matter, matting of feathers or growth in the region it indicates infections. Discharge in this region is also a sign of poor health. Bleeding or swelling is an indication of viral infections.
- Absence of solid feces in the droppings shows that the bird has some intestinal problem.
- Black droppings are a sign of internal damage and bleeding.

- Other color changes in the fecal matter which is not related to the diet of the bird is an indication of infection.
- If there is blood in your bird's dropping, it needs immediate medical attention.
- Increased fluids in the dropping indicates chances of diabetes or any such similar condition.

Even the mildest symptom should get maximum attention from your end. That is when you can ensure that your bird receives proper care at the earliest. Sometimes, it could just be a suspicion on your part that your bird is behaving differently. It is always good to clear a suspicion by visiting the vet than regretting later on for not paying enough attention to your bird.

b. Bacterial infections in Quakers

Bacterial infections are the cause for most health problems in birds. The most common bacteria that affect birds include, Staph, Strep, Citrobacter and E.Coli. These infections are mostly associated with poor sanitation, eating stale food, grit seed, and consumption of sand and unclean water. These infections are very common in birds that may have undergone stress or have a compromised immune system. So, if you have adopted a Quaker, bacterial infections could be a hazard to your bird's health. Watch out for the following signs:

- Droppings that are too watery or green in color. This is because the bacteria that has been ingested will affect the liver and kidney or irritate the bowel.
- Sneezing. This will happen if your bird has inhaled the bacterial from dust. Other dust related symptoms are rubbing of the eye, coughing, abnormal yawning, swallowing or labored breathing.
- Loss of voice or sudden change in voice.

Whether your bird has inhaled the bacteria or ingested it, your bird's health and life may be in danger. Diagnosis will help you understand which bacteria is responsible for infection. Of course, providing treatment accordingly will ensure quicker recovery for your little friend.

Treatment
The culture test is very important to determine what antibiotic is best suited for your bird. You can accordingly get injections or drops that can be orally administered to the bird. It is also possible to administer some of these antibiotics through the drinking water. Of course, in this case, you need to be sure that your bird is actually consuming enough water for the medicine to be effective enough.

The first thing to do when your bird is diagnosed with a bacterial infection is cleaning up the cage. Remove any food or food particles from the cage. Disinfect the cage thoroughly including the utensils and the toys that you have in the cage. Then, you need to start off with the diet specified by your vet. As much as possible, avoid leaving your bird out of the cage unattended. Until your bird has recovered fully, do not let him wander around the house. Some of these bacteria are also potentially hazardous to people.

Some of the commonly administered medicines are Baytril, Tylan 200 injection or Tylan Soluble. To help these medicines act faster on the infection, you can give your bird Turbobooster. It is also a good idea to provide energy supplements along with a sterile seed diet for at least three weeks. After the antibiotic cycle is over, you can even add Ioford and Dufoplus in the drinking water of your bird to prevent relapse of the infection.

Always make sure that your bird is consuming the food and water that you are providing him with. That is when you can be sure that your bird is on his way to recovery. In case of severe eating problems, you can also opt for forced feeding in a hospital.

Bacterial infections may cause long term damage to your bird if not treated soon. Some of these bacteria can harm the kidneys or the liver of your bird. Always make an effort to understand where your bird's infection originated. If you are able to figure that out, you can eliminate the source and makes sure that your bird stays healthier for longer. You must also prevent bacterial infections from recurring as they may damage your health as well. It is also a good idea to adopt a holistic approach by including herbs like goldenseal herb, licorice root or even Echinacea herb in your bird's treatment process. These are natural antibacterial agents that have long been used in the treatment of bacterial infections in birds.

If you have more than one bird at home, you need to be extra careful as these infections can spread from one bird to another through the droppings or water. As for humans, campylobacter is one type that can cause serious illnesses.

It is important for you to note that most bacterial infections are related to the environment that the bird lives in. If it is unclean and unkempt, chances are that the contamination will enter your bird through the mouth. Especially when your bird has contracted an infection in the past, you need to be extra careful with maintaining better standards of health. Here are some of the most common origins of specific bacterial infections.

E.Coli:

- Eating rotting fruit
- Sudden fluctuations in temperature
- Stress
- Wet areas in the cage
- Fungal growth in the cage
- Unhygienic environment

Strep

- Any underlying viral infection, mostly polyomavirus
- Dusty environment
- Poor quality of seed

- Stress

Staph
- Mice
- Dust
- Poor quality seed
- Poorly maintained Air Conditioning

Diplococcus:
- Stress
- Mice

Citrobacter:
- Stress
- Unclean water

Mucoid
- Unclean water
- Grout in the bathing sink

Pseudomonas
- Unclean

It is pretty evident that most of the infections in birds is due to poor sanitation. If you follow the cage maintenance ideas and tips provided in the earlier pages, you should be able to protect your bird from most diseases and infections.

c. Viral Infections
Viral infections are extremely hazardous to birds. There are certain diseases that will affect the Psittacine family that all Parrots belong to. Some of them can be diagnosed and treated. However, preventive care against viral diseases is a must because most of them manifest very fast without any symptoms and can be fatal for your beloved bird.

Avian Polyomavirus

This virus usually affects younger Parrots. Adult birds are usually immune to infections by this virus and will usually shed the virus for 90 days before any possible infection. In the young birds, this infection usually leads to death of the bird within 48 hours of contracting the virus. There are a few signs such as sudden lethargy, crop stasis, hemorrhage, distention of the abdomen and abnormalities in the feather.

If the birds are over 3 weeks old, there are chances of survival. The birds that do survive will display severe abnormalities in the feathers. It is believed that most adult Parrots are carriers of this virus. This is why quarantining is essential if you are planning to introduce a new bird into your aviary.

In case birds do show some signs, blood samples and cloacal swabs are collected to conduct tests. There are certain tests called virus neutralizing tests that are used to check if any bird has been exposed to this virus before. These tests are based on the clinical tests.

In deceased birds, hemorrhages and pale musculature is noticed. The kidneys and internal organs are usually enlarged. The only way to prevent this condition is sticking to strict hygiene procedures. It is recommended that you do not have any bird visitors in your home. When you pick a breeder to get your bird from, make sure that he also follows strict hygiene. A closed aviary system is recommended always as the birds are healthiest in such a set up. In pet stores, birds obtained from different sources must be kept away from each other. Vaccination is available for young birds that should be administered with a 2 week interval. It is best that you give the bird a shot within 35 days of birth. After 2-3 weeks, a booster shot is recommended.

Psittacine Beak and Feather Disease

PBFD is caused by psittacine circovus. This virus was discovered in the 1970s in birds like Cockatoos. Birds that are infected will shed the virus through their feces, oral secretions, feather dander and feathers. This virus can be transmitted to other birds through inhalation and ingestion.

Despite the name, beak or feather abnormality is not a clinical sign. If these signs are seen, it means that your bird is already critical. PCR tests have been used to decrease the prevalence of this condition in captive birds. This condition is usually seen when the bird is a juvenile and not so much when the bird is more than three years of age.

The most obvious sign of this disease is lack of any powder down on the beak of the bird. Growing feathers after molting will usually be abnormal. The base will be clubbed or there is hemorrhage in the shaft that is developing. The feathers are very weak and will fall easily. In birds that are as brightly colored as the Quaker, they will show obvious signs of color loss in the feathers. Skin lesions may occur and stay for a prolonged time. The progression of the disease leads to low immunity and death is usually caused by secondary infections contracted by the birds. If the virus inclusion occurs in the bone marrow, the bursa or the thymus, death occurs suddenly.

The results of the PCR tests on the blood, the dander, the feces and the feather follicles of the bird are the only sources for diagnosis. In some birds that appear quite healthy, infection may be diagnosed in these tests. These birds will respond eventually to the infection. Birds that have been tested positive for this virus should be allowed to rest and should be quarantined.

There is no treatment for this condition. You can only provide supportive care. Because it is so contagious, the birds will usually succumb to this infection. Sometimes the condition is so severe that the birds are euthanized. Strict hygiene with a lot of importance to dust control in the best preventive measure against this condition. It is recommended that you have any new bird that you introduced thoroughly checked before you introduce it to the aviary.

Pacheco's Disease

This is a herpes virus that mostly affects Parrots. This disease is seen in most new world Parrots like Quaker Parrots. This infection is mostly related to stress. A bird under stress will release this virus, causing infection in other birds that could be susceptible. There are several factors that affect the outcome of this condition. It depends on the overall health of your bird, the species and also the strength of the virus that has infected your bird. If a bird has been infected in the past, he is definitely a carrier and a potential threat to all birds that he is associated with.

The condition is terminal when you observe very bright yellow droppings with no fecal matter. There are several other sigs such as lethargy, regurgitation, diarrhea, weakness and possible depression in your bird. You can only diagnose this condition using blood samples and cloacal swabs.

Treatment for this condition is only supportive. You could administer antibiotics and analgesics to control the condition. These medicines prevent the chances of any sort of secondary infection in the bird that could lead to death in some cases.

Proventricular Dialation Disease (PDD)

This condition is also called the Macaw Wasting Disease. It was first diagnosed in birds in the USA and Germany in the year 1970. This disease is caused by a virus called the Avian Bornavirus

When a bird is affected, the first thing you will notice is sudden weight loss. Surprisingly, this weight loss is often followed by excessive eating. The undigested foods are passed through regurgitation or in the stool. You will see whole, undigested seeds in the droppings of the bird. Normally, neurological signs are observed in birds. This includes tremors, ataxia, weakness, blindness or convulsions. The progression could be slow or acute. The only thing certain about this condition is the high mortality rate.

Before the avian bornavirus was detected, crop biopsy was the common method of diagnosis. However, now PCR testing is used to diagnose the condition and check for possible chances of infection in the bird. It is still unknown how birds contract this virus.

Treatment for this condition includes providing foods that are very easy to digest. This can be aided by administering medicines like meloxicam. It is necessary to isolate a bird that has been tested positive if you have multiple birds at home. This virus does not live long in the environment. So if you are able to keep the cage and the environment of your bird clean, you can be sure that your bird will be much less prone to this condition whether you have an aviary or just an individual cage in your home. Using UV light is recommended in prevention of these viral infections.

Poxvirus infection

This is a very large strain of DNA virus. This virus is usually seen in the oral cavity, the respiratory tract and the epithelial cells of the infected bird. It is believed that all birds, irrespective of the species, are susceptible to this condition.

The type of infection depends upon the age of your bird and overall health of the bird. The common clinical signs include lesions in the larynx, pharynx and the tongue. The bird also has a very ruffled appearance. They may become depressed and anorexic. You will notice several wart like growths on the skin of the bird.

There is no specific treatment for this condition. It includes a host of treatments such as assisted feeding, topical ointments for eye and skin infections and even Vitamin A supplementation. It is possible that this virus is transmitted through mosquito bites. You may also have to clean the lesions on a daily basis. Giving the bird a lot of fluids and water is recommended to speed up the healing process. So, if you are bringing home a Parrot, it is essential that you keep pest control in mind.

d. Nutritional Diseases in Quakers

It is very important that you provide your bird with proper nutrition. This is one of the most important concerns for most pet owners, avian vets and breeders. Avian nutrition has improved greatly in the past. However, there are still several birds that are just poorly or inappropriately fed.

There are two common reasons for improper nutrition in birds. First, is giving the bird a choice in foods. If you give him a variety of foods at the same time, he is likely to only eat the foods that he likes. Second, giving them a seed only diet can also lead to malnutrition in birds.

There are various illnesses in birds that are a result of improper nutrition. Hepatic diseases, renal insufficiency, musculoskeletal conditions, respiratory issues etc. are all caused by compromised nutrition in birds. The most common nutritional diseases in birds include:

Obesity

This is very common in birds that are kept at home. Owners allow the birds to overindulge. They will feed them a seed rich diet, table foods and lots of treats. In addition to this, if your bird is not getting sufficient nutrition, he will become obese. If your Quaker is 20% over the recommended weigh and has a 4/5 keel score, he is termed obese. Quaker birds are among the highest prone pet birds to obesity. There are a few clinical sigs such as obvious fat around the belly region, inability to walk properly and strained breathing.

It is a good idea to convert these birds to a pellet diet. You also need to control the portions of the food that you give your bird. Make sure that he gets a lot of exercise with toys or even by placing multiple bowls for food. If your bird is capable of flight, you can also get him a large flight cage and leave him there for a few minutes every day. Obese birds will develop conditions like fatty liver disease, cardiac diseases and artherosclerosis.

Vitamin A Deficiency

Vitamin A is one of the most important nutrients for immunity in birds. If your bird has hypovitaminosis A, there are chances that the gastrointestinal tract, the reproductive tract and the uropygial glands of the bird are affected. The common symptoms include conjunctivitis, sneezing, polyuria, polydipsia, poor feather quality, anorexia and feather plucking. The papilla near the cloaca are also blunt or absent. You will see white plaques in the eyes, mouth and the sinuses of the bird. In chronic conditions sinusitis, pododermatitis and conjunctivitis is observed.

Treatment of this condition includes treating the secondary infections first and then providing vitamin A supplementation. The bird should be given a good pellet diet as opposed to ½ pellet and ½ seed. You can use precursors of Vitamin A in the form of sprays over the food that you give your bird. If you are doubtful about the diet of your bird, consult your avian vet or have the food that you are currently giving the bird examined for the Vitamin A content.

Iodine deficiency

If your bird is on an all seed diet, this condition is very common. With fortified diets available these days, this condition is observed very rarely in the bird. If your bird does have iodine deficiency, you will observe strained breathing, wheezing and clicking because the thyroid puts a lot of pressure on the respiratory tract of the bird. You can add a drop of Lugol's iodine in the bird's water to help him recover from this deficiency. Changing the diet will help subside the symptoms and also rebalance the iodine levels in the bird.

Phosphate, Calcium and Vitamin D3 Conditions

Commonly, birds that have a seed based diet will have an imbalance in the phosphorous, calcium and Vitamin D3 levels. You will also observe amino acid deficiency in these bird. The most commonly used treat, sunflower seeds, is very low in calcium and high in fat. Although some people may tell you otherwise, safflower seeds are more harmful for your bird as it contains large amounts of fat. It is best to give your bird a good balanced meal and ensure that he gets a lot of exercise to stay in shape.

Metabolic Bone Disease

This condition is usually observed in younger birds. It is also caused due to an imbalance in the calcium and phosphorous ration. If your bird is on a high seed diet, there is a good chance that the calcium levels will deplete drastically. Most indoor birds also fail to get enough sunlight which leads to a deficiency in the vitamin D3 levels.

Birds with this condition display deformation of the bones, the vertebrae especially. You will also observe signs like seizures, depression, weakness, ataxia, tremors and repeated fractures. If your bird is in the breeding phase, the production of eggs reduces drastically and more embryonic deaths occur.

Iron Storage Problems

When excessive iron is accumulated in the liver, several diseases may occur. When the level of iron increases, the membranes and the proteins are damaged. This condition has been seen occasionally in Quaker birds and is not as common as the other nutritional conditions. The most common clinical signs include dyspnea, ascites, depression, weight loss, distension in the abdomen etc. Usually, the heart, the liver and the spleen are most affected. This leads to several conditions like circulation failure.

Supplementing the food with fibers, tannins and phylates is best for the bird. You must also avoid Vitamin C supplementation as it causes over absorption of iron.

You also need to be careful about the brands of foods that you choose for your bird. Sometimes birds may develop conditions related to the preservatives added in the foods that you choose. Also keeping your bird physically and mentally stimulated will go a long way in ensuring that all the nutrients are properly assimilated. Try to give your bird as much natural sunlight as possible. These simple measures can prevent most of the diseases related to diet and lifestyle in birds.

e. Feather Plucking

Feather plucking is common in birds as they use the beak to groom and preen themselves often. The only time it becomes a serious issue is when the bird is actually mutilating himself in the process of plucking the feathers out. The more frequent the feather plucking, the greater the chances of the bird injuring himself. Although it is commonly termed as a behavioral problem, there are several reasons why birds begin to pluck their own feathers, such as:

- Malnutrition
- Cysts on the skin
- Parasitic infections
- Stress
- Boredom
- Cancer
- Liver disease
- Allergies to food or dust
- Inflammation of the skin
- Skin infection
- Heavy metal poisoning
- Metabolic problems
- Dryness in the skin
- Low humidity
- Lack of proper sunlight
- Any disturbance in sleep patterns
- Presence of preservatives or dyes in the food.

You may think that a bird resorts to feather plucking only when he is bored or unhappy. However, even if your bird is too exhausted with less rest, he may begin to pluck his feathers out. A bird who has the problem of feather plucking will be rather aggressive and anxious. This may be very different from the normal demeanor of your beloved bird.

Most often, birds will suddenly display feather plucking when they are ready to breed and nest.

This is also called brood patch plucking. You know that your bird is plucking due to the breeding instinct because the feathers from the abdominal region and the chest area are plucked out. This is actually done by females to be able to transfer heat during the incubation phase. If your bird is not mated, sexual urges make them pluck their feathers as they are unable to fulfil this need. Now, if your Quaker is bonded with only one person in the house, it is possible that the bird thinks of that person as the mate. When the bird's "mate" showers attention on someone else, say another pet or a new baby, feather plucking is observed.

If your bird is housed in a cage that is too small or if the perch is not comfortable, he may begin to pluck his feathers out. This is because he probably feels uncomfortable and unhappy in his space. If your bird is unable to get enough exercise or mental stimulation, he will chew on his own feathers as an attempt to keep himself entertained.

If you have trimmed the wings of your bird incorrectly, he will begin to pluck his feathers as an attempt to make the feathers more even. Quaker Parrots are very sensitive creatures. If they see a lot of emotional turmoil in their home such as constant fighting, they tend to develop anxiety. Even the smallest change in the environment such as the flickering of a light can irritate the bird enough to cause feather plucking.

This can be a really frustrating time for you as well as the bird, and he may develop habits like chewing, biting, over preening etc. In order to curb this issue you need to be extremely patient with your bird and first get to the root of the problem. Understand why the bird is behaving in this manner. If you are unable to figure that out for yourself, you can also visit the vet for a consultation.

There are some measures that you can take to help alleviate this issue:

- Keep your bird mentally stimulated
- If he is plucking for attention, make sure that you do not give in to it. Instead, giving him an out time when he starts plucking tells him that plucking does not get your attention.
- Make sure that the food you give your bird is healthy and adequate.
- Get the feathers clipped by a professional.
- Make sure you have regular health checkups for your bird.
- The day and night lighting should be consistent. If your bird is in a room that has a TV, you might want to give him a sleeping tent so that he can get enough rest.

The problem with feather plucking is that it is not easy to fix. Your bird will always have a tendency to pluck once he begins. Also, the rate of feather plucking and the duration depends on the cause. For example, if it is because of an infection, you can give him medicines and feather plucking will subside eventually. However, if feather plucking occurs after you got married and your bird is jealous of your spouse, it may take a lot of time for him to give this habit up. On your part, you need to be patient. If you feel like you are unable to help your bird, you can look for assistance from your avian vet. Follow all the instructions precisely and it is possible that your bird will recover soon. The best remedy for feather plucking is preventive care and ensuring that your bird is always healthy and happy.

Feather plucking v/s molting

In particular seasons, you may find several feathers on the floor of your bird's cage. You will also notice bald patches on the bird's body. This is not a cause for concern as the bird has started molting. Usually, Quakers begin to molt at the age of 4 months.

Feather plucking is the voluntary removal of feathers and consequently mutilating the body. Molting, on the other hand, is a natural and seasonal process that allows your bird to shed old feathers and grow new ones.

A bird that is molting will be irritable and grumpy, as this is a very uncomfortable phase for the bird. You can help by misting the feathers to relieve itching and burning sensations. You may also change the diet of the bird after consulting the vet to make the molting process less painful for the bird.

f. Accidents and Injuries

Unlike other pets like cats and dogs, even the simplest injury to a bird can be life threatening. The reason for this is that birds go into shock very easily. And, when this occurs, the cardiovascular system of the bird does not function properly, leading to a loss of blood flow to the vital organs. That is why, the first step towards treating any injury or trauma to the bird is helping him calm down. If you see that your bird has had an accident, take him to a quiet room and leave him there with some water. Make sure that you do not panic or scream in front of the bird. This makes it worse for him. Let him calm down and then you can talk to him in a calm and comforting voice. Of course, if the injury is serious, you need to take the bird to the vet immediately. Here are some common accidents that your bird may encounter and the necessary measures you have to take:

- **Skin wounds:** If the bird has cuts or bruises on the skin, wash it gently with 3% hydrogen peroxide. You can use gauze, q-tips or cotton to clean the area. In case the skin wound is caused by a cat or dog bite, wash the area and rush the bird to a vet. In order to stop bleeding in the skin, you can use a styptic pencil or you can also use cornstarch.
- **Bleeding nail or beak:** Sometimes, the bird's beak or nail can get entangled in the wires used to hang toys. It could also get caught in the bars of the cage. Then, you need to apply pressure on the injured area directly using a paper towel or cotton gauze. If that is not good enough, you can use a styptic pencil or cornstarch to control bleeding.

- **Broken blood feathers:** Bleeding in the broken blood feathers is profuse and can even be fatal if you do not curb bleeding immediately. Use a styptic pencil to clot blood and hold the area down with a gauze or clean tissue paper.
- **Burns:** If your bird suffers from burns due to a hot stove, hot water, steam or even hot utensils, you can relieve the pain by misting the feathers with cold water. If the leg or foot is burnt, just dip it in cold water. Make sure that the water is not too cold. It should be cold water from the tap, not the refrigerator. You can use an antibiotic cream. But make sure that it is not oil or grease based as the heat is retained by such creams. In case of acid burns due to cleaning agents or detergents, flood the area with lots of cold water to relieve the pain.
- **Heatstroke:** The best thing to do would be to put the bird in an air-conditioned room. If you do not use air conditioning in your home, you can use cold water to mist the feathers and then turn on a fan. If you are turning a fan on, make sure that the bird is in a cage. Then, give the bird water to drink. In case of extreme heat strokes, it might become necessary to drop water into the bird's mouth directly.
- **Broken bones or wings:** It is best that you do not handle a bird with broken bones. This may happen by flying into a window, predator attacks, getting caught between a door etc. In case of a broken wing, you can hold the wing close to the body and secure it before transferring the bird to a travel cage. You need to remove any perch or toy from the cage if you are transporting a bird with broken bones. Line the floor with a soft towel with no loops to keep the bird secure throughout the journey.

In case of any emergency, you can contact:
- In USA, ASPCA- 1-888-4-ANI-HELP
- In UK, RSPCA- 0844-453-0117

These services will provide you with immediate care for your bird. When you are not sure how to deal with a situation, it is best that you either give them a call or give your vet a call. If you are unsure about handling an emergency, you can make the situation worse for your bird. The only thing you need to do then is make sure that you stay calm and keep other people away from the bird till you are able to get some help.

g. First Aid Kit for Birds

In order to provide timely care for your bird in case of an emergency, you need to have an emergency kit ready at all times. Here are a few things that you must include in your first aid kit:

- A blood coagulant: This helps prevent any profuse bleeding. A styptic pencil is the best option. If that is not available, you may use cornstarch or even flour.
- Tweezers: The bandages that you use for your bird will be very small in size. Having a pair of tweezers makes it easier for you to handle them.
- Cotton swabs: Any time you need to clean up a wound, cotton swabs will come in very handy. If you do not have any, you can even use Q-tips.
- Gauze: You need gauze to clean and wrap cuts, bruises and even bites. Sometimes, it also helps secure broken wings or bones.
- Bandages: If you want to have bandages in your bird's first aid box, make sure that they are non-adhesive. Specialized bandages are available for birds in most pet stores.
- Syringe: You will need a syringe to wash small wounds or the eyes of the bird.
- Disinfectants: The best option is hydrogen peroxide as it removes any germs that might cause infections to your bird.
- Towel: An injured bird can get aggressive and irritated. So using a towel to handle him will make things a lot easier for you.

Keeping a first aid kit handy is important. Also make sure that you are checking the contents for cleanliness and hygiene. If you notice that the bandages are dirty or dusty, replace them immediately. If not, your bird may develop secondary infections that are harder to deal with than the actual injury itself.

h. Preventive care

There is no better way to keep your bird healthy than preventive care. Since most illnesses spread so fast in Quaker birds, it is best that you take all the precautionary steps possible to prevent this sort of infection in the first place. Here are some tips that will help you maintain the health of your little feathered companion:

- Make sure that the diet is wholesome and nutritious
- Clean the cage and its contents regularly
- Take your pet to the vet for an annual checkup without fail
- Any new bird that is introduced to your home must be quarantined without fail
- The bird must have a lot of clean water to drink
- Your Quaker must be mentally stimulated in order to ensure good health
- Spend enough time with your bird to prevent any behavioral problems
- You need to make sure that he gets ample sunlight. It is a good idea to take the bird outdoors provided he is harnessed or is protected by a cage.
- Your home must be bird proofed even before you bring the bird home.
- Grooming and cleaning the bird is necessary.

Always keep your vet's number handy and learn as much as you can about your Quaker's health. That way, communicating with the vet also becomes easier and you will be able to provide better care for your bird.

Chapter 10: What are the Expenses?

The one thing that all new bird owners forget about is the financial commitment. This is, in fact, the most important part of raising your Parrot. The minimum expenses include:

- **Cost of the bird:** If you decide to adopt a Quaker Parrot, it will cost you approximately $150 or £75. If you buy a bird from a breeder or a pet store, it will cost you about $350-400 or £150-200.
- **Cost of the cage:** You must never compromise on the quality of the cage and ensure that your bird gets nothing but the best. A good cage will cost you about $180-400 or £100-200. It should be made from good material and should be secure for the bird.
- **Food Expenses:** It is necessary to give your Parrot a good mixture of fresh produce and pellets. Of course, you need to add treats as well. If you add up all the costs, it will come up to at least $50 or £30 each month.
- **Veterinary costs:** Veterinary costs will go up to $1200 or £800 annually. On an average, every consultation should cost you close to $50 or £30.
- **Toys:** You need to keep buying new toys to keep a Quaker entertained. You can expect to spend at least $30 or £15 each month on the toys alone.
- **Insurance:** As discussed before, insurance can cost up to $250 or £150 each month depending upon the coverage that you opt for.

On an average you could spend close to $400 or £200 each month on bird care. Before you bring a bird home, make sure that you take this sum out of your monthly income and put it away. If you are able to manage all your expenses for the month and if you can keep this up for at least three months, you are ready for the financial commitment of a Quaker. If not you may have to wait a little longer or figure out how you will manage these expenses.

Conclusion

I hope that you have had fun reading this book and understanding all the nuances of bird care.

Having an intelligent creature like the Parrot can be overwhelming at times. So, we have compiled all the information that you will need, even if you are a beginner in the world of Parrots.

Here is wishing you an amazing journey with your Parrot friend.

References

Note: at the time of printing, all the websites below were working. As the internet changes rapidly, some sites might no longer be live when you read this book. That is, of course, out of our control.

You may refer to the following websites for more information on your Quaker Parrot:

www.birdchannel.com

www.webvet.com

www.quakerParrots.com

www.birdtricks.com

www.birdsnways.com

www.vcahospitals.com

www.angelfire.com

www.beautyofbirds.com

http://www.sissysbirdcolony.com/

http://birds.about.com/

http://www.onegreenplanet.org/

http://www.featherme.com/

http://www.companionParrots.org/

http://birdsbyjoe.com/

http://www.merckvetmanual.com/

http://www.peteducation.com/

http://www.webvet.com/

http://www.Parrotscanada.com/

https://www.kellyvillepets.com.au

http://www.pets4homes.co.uk/

www.Parrotsecrets.com

forums.avianavenue.com

www.talkingquakerParrot.com

www.quakerquaker.org

www.quakerParrotforum.com

www.Parrotforums.com

www.Parrotdebate.com

www.tailfeathersnetwork.com

www.mothering.com

www.reptile-Parrots.com

www.theParrotclub.co.uk

www.Parrots.org

Made in the USA
Coppell, TX
12 May 2021